Empowerment and Independence

A Training Guide For Job Development And Retention Coaches
Supporting Neurodiverse Individuals

NIALL W. BROWNE

Table of Contents

Introduction

Purpose of the Book

The book "Embracing Differences: Career Coaching for Neurodiverse Individuals" aims to serve as a comprehensive guide for career coaches, educators, human resources professionals, and others involved in supporting the career development of neurodiverse individuals. It primarily focuses on career coaching and development for individuals with neurodiverse conditions such as autism spectrum disorder, ADHD, dyslexia, and others.

Neurodiversity denotes the natural variation in the human brain, advocating that neurological differences should be acknowledged and respected rather than stigmatized or viewed as disorders. Neurodiverse individuals possess unique strengths, skills, and perspectives that can significantly enrich workplace environments. Nonetheless, they often encounter challenges in conventional career development processes, including job interviews, networking, and workplace interactions.

The book's objective is to empower career coaches and professionals to effectively support neurodiverse individuals in their career journeys. It provides practical strategies, tools, and resources to help these professionals comprehend the specific needs and strengths of neurodiverse individuals, customize their coaching approaches, and establish inclusive career development programs.

Throughout the book, readers will gain insights into various neurodiverse conditions, their impact on career development, and the hurdles neurodiverse individuals may confront. They will also learn to identify and leverage the strengths of neurodiverse individuals, such as attention to detail, problem-solving abilities, and creativity.

The book also explores the significance of cultivating inclusive and supportive work environments for neurodiverse individuals. It offers guidance on fostering understanding, acceptance, and accommodation within organizations, as well as promoting diversity and inclusion initiatives.

By reading "Embracing Differences: Career Coaching for Neurodiverse Individuals," career coaches, educators, human resources professionals, and others involved in supporting the career development of neurodiverse individuals will gain the knowledge, skills, and confidence to guide their clients toward fulfilling and successful careers. They will be equipped to embrace the unique strengths and differences of neurodiverse individuals and assist them in thriving in the workplace.

Overview of Neurodiversity and Career Development

Neurodiversity encompasses the understanding that neurological differences, such as autism, ADHD, dyslexia, and other neurodevelopmental conditions, are natural variations of the human brain rather than deficits or disorders. This recognition has garnered significant attention in recent years, prompting a shift in societal perceptions and support for individuals with neurodiverse traits. In the context of career development, embracing neurodiversity involves recognizing and valuing the unique strengths and abilities that neurodiverse individuals bring to the workplace.

This section provides an overview of neurodiversity and its implications for career coaching and development. It is specifically tailored for career coaches, educators, human resources professionals, and others involved in supporting the career journeys of neurodiverse individuals.

The first segment delves deeper into the concept of neurodiversity, highlighting the spectrum of neurodiverse conditions and the typically associated strengths. Emphasis is placed on reframing neurodiversity as an asset rather than a limitation, fostering a more inclusive and supportive work environment.

The subsequent segment addresses the distinct challenges that neurodiverse individuals may encounter in their career development. It discusses common barriers, such as social communication difficulties, sensory sensitivities, executive functioning challenges, and workplace transition difficulties. Practical strategies and accommodations to surmount these challenges are presented, empowering career coaches and support professionals to better assist neurodiverse individuals in their career journeys.

The third segment focuses on the role of career coaching in supporting the career development of neurodiverse individuals. It outlines specific coaching techniques and approaches that have proven effective in empowering and guiding neurodiverse individuals toward their professional goals. These approaches may include strengths-based assessments, personalized career planning, skill-building exercises, and self-advocacy training.

Additionally, this section offers insights into the importance of nurturing self-confidence, self-awareness, and self-advocacy skills among neurodiverse individuals. It underscores the significance of cultivating an inclusive and accepting workplace culture that values diversity and provides reasonable accommodations for individuals with neurodiverse traits.

In conclusion, this section aims to equip career coaches, educators, human resources professionals, and others involved in supporting the career development of neurodiverse individuals with a comprehensive understanding of neurodiversity and its impact on career coaching and development. By embracing neurodiversity and providing tailored support, these professionals can empower neurodiverse individuals to achieve their full potential and thrive in their chosen careers.

Importance of Tailored Coaching Approaches

In the realm of career coaching and development for neurodiverse individuals, the significance of tailored coaching approaches cannot be overstated. Neurodiverse individuals, encompassing those with autism, ADHD, dyslexia, and other neurological differences, possess unique strengths, challenges, and diverse ways of processing information. Consequently, employing a one-size-fits-all coaching approach is unlikely to yield optimal results for this demographic.

Tailored coaching approaches are crucial for neurodiverse individuals due to the necessity of accommodating their varied learning styles and communication preferences. Traditional coaching methods often heavily rely on verbal communication and written exercises, posing challenges for individuals with language processing difficulties or sensory sensitivities. By customizing coaching approaches to integrate visual aids, hands-on activities, and alternative communication methods, coaches can establish a more inclusive and supportive environment, enabling neurodiverse individuals to flourish.

Another pivotal aspect of tailored coaching approaches involves recognizing and harnessing the unique strengths and talents of neurodiverse individuals. Despite facing certain workplace challenges like social interaction difficulties or attention to detail issues, these individuals often excel in areas such as pattern recognition, problem-solving, and creative thinking. By identifying and leveraging these strengths, coaches can assist neurodiverse individuals in discovering career paths and roles that resonate with their abilities and interests, fostering greater job satisfaction and success.

Moreover, tailored coaching approaches address the specific challenges neurodiverse individuals may encounter in the workplace. This may entail providing strategies for managing sensory overload, developing coping mechanisms for stress and anxiety, or enhancing executive functioning skills such as time management and organization. Customizing the coaching process to tackle these challenges empowers neurodiverse individuals, enabling them to navigate the workplace confidently and independently.

Ultimately, the essence of tailored coaching approaches lies in their capacity to nurture empowerment and independence among neurodiverse individuals. By comprehending and accommodating their unique needs, strengths, and challenges, coaches can cultivate a supportive and inclusive environment conducive to personal growth and career success. For career coaches, educators, human resources professionals, and others involved in supporting the career development of neurodiverse individuals, embracing tailored coaching approaches is crucial to ensure every individual has the opportunity to achieve their full potential and thrive in the workplace.

CHAPTER 1

Understanding Neurodiversity

Defining Neurodiversity

To effectively coach and support neurodiverse individuals in their career development, understanding the essence of neurodiversity is essential. Neurodiversity embodies the natural variation of neurological differences among the human population. It acknowledges that individuals with diverse neurological profiles, such as autism, ADHD, dyslexia, and others, possess unique strengths, abilities, and information processing methods.

Neurodiversity challenges the conventional perception that neurological differences indicate disorders or deficits needing correction or normalization. Instead, it celebrates the diversity of human brains and acknowledges that these distinctions offer valuable perspectives, skills, and contributions to workplaces. By embracing neurodiversity, inclusive environments are cultivated, enabling neurodiverse individuals to thrive and contribute their unique talents.

Understanding neurodiversity also means recognizing it as a spectrum. Each individual's encounter with neurodiversity is distinct, with varying degrees of challenges and strengths. For career coaches, educators, human resources professionals, and others supporting neurodiverse individuals, adopting a person-centered approach is crucial. This approach involves comprehending and appreciating an individual's specific neurodivergent traits, strengths, and challenges, tailoring support to meet their requirements.

Neurodiversity challenges the notion of a "one-size-fits-all" approach to career coaching and development. Traditional methods and strategies may not suit neurodiverse individuals, who often benefit from accommodations, adjustments, or alternative approaches to reach their full potential. Hence, flexibility and openness to innovative solutions are essential for career coaches and professionals supporting neurodiverse individuals.

Embracing neurodiversity empowers career coaches and professionals to unlock the full potential of neurodiverse individuals, aiding in their career success and meaningful contributions to workplaces. This subchapter further explores the concept of neurodiversity, examining its facets and implications for career coaching and development. It offers practical strategies, tools, and resources for effective support in the career journeys of neurodiverse individuals. Through a comprehensive understanding of neurodiversity, an environment inclusive and empowering to all individuals, irrespective of their neurological differences, can be fostered.

Common Neurodiverse Conditions

In this subchapter, we explore some prevalent neurodiverse conditions encountered by career coaches, educators, human resources professionals, and others supporting the career development of neurodiverse individuals. Understanding these conditions is pivotal in effectively coaching and empowering neurodiverse individuals for career success.

Autism Spectrum Disorder (ASD): ASD involves difficulties in social interaction, communication, and repetitive behaviors. Individuals with ASD might excel in attention to detail, problem-solving, and creativity, yet face challenges in social interactions and adapting to workplace changes.

Attention-Deficit/Hyperactivity Disorder (ADHD): ADHD manifests as difficulties in sustaining attention, hyperactivity, and impulsivity. Individuals with ADHD might struggle with time management, organization, and maintaining focus, but often possess high energy levels, creativity, and unconventional thinking.

Dyslexia: Dyslexia affects reading and language processing. Individuals with dyslexia may have trouble with reading, writing, spelling, and comprehension, yet exhibit strengths in problem-solving, critical thinking, and verbal communication.

Dyspraxia: Dyspraxia impacts motor coordination and planning skills. Individuals with dyspraxia might face challenges in fine motor skills and task organization but often display excellent problem-solving abilities and creativity.

Tourette Syndrome: Tourette Syndrome involves involuntary repetitive movements or vocalizations known as tics. Individuals with Tourette Syndrome might struggle to control their tics, affecting social interactions and workplace dynamics, yet exhibit high intelligence, creativity, and perseverance.

Anxiety and Depression: While not exclusive to neurodiverse individuals, anxiety and depression are common co-occurring conditions that significantly impact self-esteem, motivation, and workplace navigation.

Familiarizing themselves with these common neurodiverse conditions allows career coaches, educators, human resources professionals, and others to better comprehend the unique strengths and challenges faced by neurodiverse individuals. This knowledge enables them to tailor coaching strategies and support mechanisms for neurodiverse individuals to thrive in their careers.

Throughout this book, each of these conditions will be explored in depth, analyzing their impact on career development and offering practical strategies to empower and guide neurodiverse individuals. By embracing these differences and providing requisite support, the career success and fulfillment of neurodiverse individuals in a diverse and inclusive society can be facilitated.

Autism Spectrum Disorder

Autism Spectrum Disorder (ASD) is a complex neurodevelopmental condition impacting an individual's social skills, communication abilities, and behavioral patterns. It encompasses a wide range of symptoms and levels of impairment, rendering each person with ASD unique. This subchapter aims to provide career coaches, educators, human resources professionals, and others supporting the career development of neurodiverse individuals with an extensive understanding of ASD and its influence on career choices and success.

Understanding the Autism Spectrum:

ASD is a spectrum disorder, encompassing a wide range of symptoms and abilities. Some individuals with ASD may encounter significant difficulties with communication and social interaction, while others possess exceptional skills in certain areas. Recognizing this diversity is crucial for career coaches and other professionals to tailor their support accordingly.

Challenges and Strengths:

Individuals with ASD may encounter specific workplace challenges such as social cues, sensory sensitivities, and executive functioning skills. However, it's equally essential to recognize their unique strengths, like attention to detail, reliability, and strong task focus. Career coaches should assist individuals with ASD in identifying and leveraging these strengths for fulfilling and successful careers.

Supporting Career Development:

Supporting the career development of individuals with ASD involves strategies such as creating structured environments, offering clear instructions, and fostering opportunities for social skill enhancement. Collaboration with employers to create inclusive workplaces embracing neurodiversity and providing necessary accommodations is vital.

Navigating the Job Search:

This subchapter will also address critical aspects of the job search for individuals with ASD, from resume writing and interview preparation to disclosing their neurodiversity. Guiding individuals with ASD on self-advocacy and disclosure empowers them to make informed decisions on sharing their diagnosis with employers.

Case Studies and Success Stories:

To illustrate concepts discussed, this subchapter will include real-life case studies and success stories of neurodiverse individuals who've overcome challenges and achieved career success. These stories serve as inspiration for career coaches and other professionals, demonstrating the potential and capabilities of individuals with ASD.

Conclusion

In conclusion, this subchapter on Autism Spectrum Disorder provides valuable insights and practical strategies for career coaches, educators, human resources professionals, and others involved in supporting the career development of neurodiverse individuals. Understanding the unique challenges and strengths of individuals with ASD and providing tailored support and guidance enables these professionals to empower individuals with ASD in embracing their differences and achieving fulfilling careers.

Certainly, here's an edited version of the text while preserving its original meaning:

Attention Deficit Hyperactivity Disorder (ADHD)

Understanding ADHD is critical for career coaches, educators, human resources professionals, and others involved in supporting the career development of neurodiverse individuals. ADHD, a neurodevelopmental disorder affecting both children and adults, is characterized by symptoms of inattention, hyperactivity, and impulsivity, significantly impacting an individual's ability to succeed in various aspects of life, including their career.

Individuals with ADHD often struggle to maintain focus and attention, challenging their completion of tasks, organizational skills, and meeting deadlines. Additionally, they may display impulsive behaviors, hindering their ability to consider consequences before acting. These challenges manifest in academic settings, job interviews, and professional relationships.

However, it's crucial to recognize that ADHD isn't a barrier to success but rather a distinct cognitive approach. With appropriate support and strategies, individuals with ADHD can excel in their careers. As a career coach, understanding the unique strengths and challenges of neurodiverse individuals with ADHD is vital in helping them unlock their full potential.

When coaching individuals with ADHD, providing structure and organization is crucial. Breaking tasks into smaller steps aids in maintaining focus and motivation. Encouraging tools like calendars, to-do lists, and reminders supports their organizational skills.

Moreover, assisting individuals with ADHD in developing self-awareness and self-advocacy skills is essential. Understanding their strengths and challenges empowers better communication with employers and colleagues, fostering more effective working relationships.

Furthermore, coaching should focus on identifying and leveraging their unique strengths. Many individuals with ADHD possess exceptional creativity, problem-solving abilities, and high energy levels. Harnessing these strengths can help them excel in careers requiring innovative thinking, adaptability, and fast-paced environments.

In conclusion, ADHD, a neurodevelopmental disorder, presents unique challenges and strengths for neurodiverse individuals in their career development. Understanding the nature of ADHD and offering tailored coaching strategies empower individuals with ADHD to succeed in their chosen careers. Embracing differences and strengths among neurodiverse individuals is crucial in unlocking their full potential and achieving career success.

Dyslexia

Dyslexia, a neurodevelopmental disorder impacting reading, writing, and spelling abilities, is among the most prevalent learning disabilities, affecting approximately 10% of the population to varying degrees. Within the realm of career coaching for neurodiverse individuals, understanding dyslexia is vital for offering effective support and guidance.

Individuals with dyslexia commonly encounter challenges in academic and professional settings due to difficulties processing language-based information. However, it's important to note that dyslexia doesn't indicate a lack of intelligence or potential. In reality, many individuals with dyslexia exhibit exceptional strengths in problem-solving, creativity, and critical thinking.

For career coaches, educators, and HR professionals, adopting a strengths-based approach when working with individuals with dyslexia is essential. Recognizing and leveraging their unique abilities can help unlock their full potential, enabling them to excel in their chosen careers.

Implementing practical strategies and accommodations in the workplace can support individuals with dyslexia. This includes providing alternative formats for written communication like visual aids or audio recordings to enhance comprehension. Breaking complex tasks into manageable steps and employing multi-sensory learning techniques also facilitates learning and skill development.

Additionally, creating a supportive and inclusive work environment is crucial for individuals with dyslexia to thrive. Educating colleagues and supervisors about dyslexia fosters understanding and empathy. Encouraging open communication and offering reasonable accommodations, such as flexible work hours or assistive technology, can foster a more inclusive workplace culture.

Integrating assistive technology tools into career coaching and development programs can significantly benefit individuals with dyslexia. Technologies like speech-to-text software and mind mapping tools enhance productivity, organization, and communication skills.

Ultimately, embracing the differences and unique strengths of individuals with dyslexia is pivotal for empowering their career success. By providing tailored support, accommodations, and fostering an inclusive work environment, career coaches, educators, and HR professionals can assist neurodiverse individuals with dyslexia in overcoming challenges and realizing their full potential in the workforce.

Dyspraxia

Dyspraxia: Navigating Challenges and Unlocking Potential

Introduction:

Empowering and supporting neurodiverse individuals in their career development necessitates understanding the diverse challenges they may confront. Dyspraxia, also known as Developmental Coordination Disorder (DCD), is one such challenge impacting coordination and motor skills. In this subchapter, we'll delve into dyspraxia, its influence on individuals' professional lives, and strategies aiding them to navigate and excel in their careers.

Understanding Dyspraxia:

Dyspraxia, a neurological condition affecting movement and coordination, presents challenges in fine and gross motor skills, balance, and spatial awareness. These difficulties can manifest in handwriting, task organization, and participation in activities requiring precise movements.

Impact on Career Development:

In the workplace, dyspraxia poses unique obstacles for individuals, hindering tasks requiring manual dexterity or strict deadlines due to time management and organization challenges. Moreover, dyspraxia can impact social interactions, complicating networking, relationship-building, and effective navigation of office environments.

Coaching Strategies for Supporting Individuals with Dyspraxia:

Assessment and Individualized Plans: Conduct comprehensive assessments to identify specific dyspraxia-related difficulties, tailoring coaching plans to leverage strengths and address challenges.

Skill Enhancement: Focus on developing compensatory strategies to overcome motor skill difficulties, utilizing assistive technologies, breaking tasks into smaller steps, or implementing time-management techniques.

Building Confidence: Encourage individuals to recognize and celebrate their unique strengths beyond motor challenges, fostering a positive self-image by highlighting their talents and abilities.

Workplace Accommodations: Collaborate with employers to implement reasonable accommodations supporting individuals with dyspraxia, such as flexible work hours, assistive technology, or workspace modifications.

Social Skills Training: Offer guidance on improving social interactions and communication skills through role-playing exercises, group discussions, and workshops to enhance interpersonal relationships at work.

Conclusion

Dyspraxia may pose career development hurdles for neurodiverse individuals. However, with the right support and coaching strategies, individuals with dyspraxia can thrive professionally. By embracing their unique strengths, providing tailored coaching, and advocating for workplace accommodations, career coaches, educators, and HR professionals play a pivotal role in empowering neurodiverse individuals with dyspraxia to succeed in their careers.

Tourette Syndrome

Tourette Syndrome (TS) is a neurodevelopmental disorder characterized by involuntary movements and vocalizations known as tics. It's estimated that approximately 1 in 100 people worldwide live with TS, making it more prevalent than commonly recognized. While TS presents challenges, individuals with this condition possess unique strengths that can be harnessed for career success.

Professionals involved in supporting the career development of neurodiverse individuals, including career coaches, educators, and human resources experts, must understand the specific needs and potential of those with TS. By comprehending the intricacies of this condition, these professionals can provide the necessary guidance and support to help individuals with TS embrace their differences and succeed in their chosen careers.

Challenges Posed by TS:

Individuals with TS encounter challenges due to tics, which can be both motor (such as blinking, head jerking, or shoulder shrugging) and vocal (such as throat clearing, coughing, or repeating words/phrases). These tics can be misunderstood by others as intentional or disruptive behavior, leading to misunderstandings and stigmatization.

Leveraging Strengths of Individuals with TS:

However, despite these challenges, individuals with TS often exhibit remarkable creativity, problem-solving skills, and attention to detail. These strengths can be particularly valuable in careers like graphic design, computer programming, research, and engineering. By recognizing and harnessing these strengths, career coaches can assist individuals with TS in identifying and pursuing career paths aligned with their abilities and interests.

Support Strategies for Individuals with TS in the Workplace:

Moreover, career coaches can offer strategies and accommodations to help individuals with TS manage their tics in the workplace. This may include creating a quiet workspace, implementing flexible work schedules, or utilizing assistive technologies. By tailoring these accommodations to the individual's specific needs, career coaches can help individuals with TS thrive in their work environments.

Conclusion

In conclusion, Tourette Syndrome poses unique challenges and strengths. Through understanding the specific needs of individuals with TS and capitalizing on their strengths, career coaches, educators, and human resources professionals play a vital role in supporting the career development and success of neurodiverse individuals. By fostering inclusive work environments and providing appropriate accommodations, professionals can empower individuals with TS to embrace their differences and achieve their career aspirations.

Understanding Neurodiversity and Strengths

In the realm of career coaching and development for neurodiverse individuals, comprehending the essence of neurodiversity and its connection to their distinct strengths is paramount. Neurodiversity stands as a paradigm that acknowledges and celebrates the inherent variations in the human brain, encompassing conditions like autism, ADHD, dyslexia, and others. Instead of perceiving these differences as deficiencies or disorders, neurodiversity champions the notion that these variations are integral aspects of the diverse human experience.

A fundamental aspect of embracing neurodiversity involves recognizing and harnessing the strengths inherent in neurodiverse individuals. While they might encounter challenges in certain domains, these individuals often possess exceptional abilities in others. By emphasizing these strengths, career coaches can aid neurodiverse individuals in unlocking their full potential and attaining success in their chosen careers.

Strengths manifest diversely, contingent upon the individual and their neurodivergent condition. For instance, individuals with autism may showcase exceptional attention to detail, robust pattern recognition skills, and a penchant for innovative thinking. Those with ADHD might excel in tasks demanding quick thinking, multitasking, and adaptability. Dyslexic individuals often exhibit heightened creativity, excellent problem-solving prowess, and a distinctive perspective on intricate issues.

Identifying these strengths constitutes a pivotal phase in the career coaching process. By comprehending the specific strengths of each neurodiverse individual, coaches can tailor their guidance to assist them in discovering fulfilling career paths that resonate with their innate abilities. Furthermore, coaches can aid individuals in devising strategies to leverage their strengths within the workplace, fostering a positive and empowering work environment.

Alongside recognizing individual strengths, it is imperative for career coaches to advocate for a culture of acceptance and inclusion in the workplace. By educating employers and colleagues about neurodiversity, coaches can help establish an environment that esteems the unique contributions of neurodiverse individuals. This can lead to heightened job satisfaction, enhanced productivity, and a more diverse and innovative workforce overall.

In conclusion, the concept of neurodiversity and strengths forms the cornerstone of success in career coaching and development for neurodiverse individuals. By embracing neurodiversity and accentuating the strengths of these individuals, career coaches can steer them toward gratifying careers that capitalize on their distinctive abilities. Together, we can forge a more inclusive and equitable workforce that esteems and celebrates neurodiversity.

The Importance of Embracing Differences

Subchapter: The Importance of Embracing Differences

In today's diverse and inclusive world, it is crucial for career coaches, educators, human resources professionals, and others involved in supporting the career development of neurodiverse individuals to understand and embrace the importance of differences. This subchapter aims to explore the significance of embracing neurodiversity and its positive impact on career success.

Neurodiversity refers to the natural variation in neurological differences among individuals. It encompasses a wide range of conditions such as autism, ADHD, dyslexia, and other cognitive differences. Instead of viewing these differences as disabilities, the concept of neurodiversity recognizes them as unique characteristics that contribute to the richness of human diversity.

Embracing neurodiversity in the workplace is essential for several reasons. Firstly, it promotes innovation and creativity. Neurodiverse individuals often possess exceptional skills in areas such as pattern recognition, problem-solving, and attention to detail. By embracing these differences, organizations can tap into their untapped potential and foster a culture of innovation that drives success.

Secondly, embracing neurodiversity leads to increased employee engagement and satisfaction. When organizations create an inclusive environment where neurodiverse individuals feel valued, supported, and understood, they are more likely to thrive in their careers. This, in turn, enhances job satisfaction, productivity, and overall employee well-being.

Furthermore, embracing neurodiversity contributes to a more inclusive society. By recognizing and accommodating the diverse needs and abilities of neurodiverse individuals, we break down barriers and promote equal opportunities for all. This not only benefits the individuals themselves but also leads to a more diverse and inclusive workforce, which is known to foster creativity, problem-solving, and better decision-making.

To effectively embrace differences, career coaches, educators, and human resources professionals need to adopt a person-centered approach. This involves understanding and appreciating the unique strengths, challenges, and preferences of neurodiverse individuals. By tailoring career coaching and development strategies to meet their specific needs, professionals in these fields can empower neurodiverse individuals to reach their full potential and achieve career success.

In conclusion, embracing differences in neurodiversity is of utmost importance in the context of career coaching and development for neurodiverse individuals. By recognizing and valuing their unique strengths and abilities, organizations can foster innovation, enhance employee engagement and satisfaction, and contribute to a more inclusive society. As career coaches, educators, and human resources professionals, it is our responsibility to embrace neurodiversity and empower neurodiverse individuals to thrive in their careers.

CHAPTER 2

The Role of Career Coaching for Neurodiverse Individuals

Understanding the Challenges

Effectively supporting the career development of neurodiverse individuals hinges upon a profound comprehension of the unique challenges they encounter. Although each individual's experiences differ, several common obstacles mark the career journeys of neurodiverse individuals. Recognizing and addressing these challenges empowers career coaches, educators, human resources professionals, and others in providing the requisite guidance and resources for their success.

Navigating the social aspects of the workplace stands as a primary challenge for neurodiverse individuals. Many on the autism spectrum, for instance, grapple with social interactions, impeding their capacity to build relationships and establish rapport with colleagues and supervisors. This impedes networking, collaboration, and career progression. Career coaches play a vital role by offering strategies to improve social skills, nurturing inclusive environments, and fostering understanding among peers.

Managing sensory sensitivities in the workplace presents another significant challenge. Neurodiverse individuals often contend with heightened sensory perceptions, easily overwhelmed by bright lights, loud noises, or strong smells. This poses difficulties in open office settings or roles demanding frequent travel or exposure to stimulating environments. Coaches collaborate with employers to devise sensory-friendly workspaces and tailored accommodations meeting individual needs.

Executive functioning difficulties represent a substantial hurdle for many neurodiverse individuals, manifesting in time management, organization, and task prioritization challenges. Career coaches equip individuals with strategies and tools to handle their workload effectively, set goals, and maintain organization. Moreover, coaches collaborate with employers to offer flexible work schedules and supplementary support when necessary.

Addressing the stigma and misconceptions surrounding neurodiversity in the workplace is pivotal. Discrimination, bias, and misunderstanding often plague neurodiverse individuals, fostering isolation, diminished self-esteem, and reduced job satisfaction. By promoting awareness and education, career coaches foster inclusive workplaces conducive to the thriving of neurodiverse individuals.

Understanding and tackling the challenges that neurodiverse individuals encounter in their careers are indispensable for their overall success and well-being. Equipping career coaches, educators, human resources professionals, and other stakeholders supporting neurodiverse individuals with knowledge and tools to navigate these challenges serves to empower and enable them to realize their full potential in the workplace.

Communication and Social Skills

Effective communication and strong social skills are crucial for success in any career. For neurodiverse individuals, who may face unique challenges in these areas, it is even more important to provide them with tailored support and guidance. In this subchapter, we will explore the significance of communication and social skills in the context of career coaching for neurodiverse individuals.

Communication skills encompass both verbal and non-verbal forms of expression. Neurodiverse individuals may struggle with certain aspects of communication, such as interpreting social cues, maintaining eye contact, or understanding metaphors. As career coaches, it is essential to work closely with these individuals to help them develop strategies to overcome these challenges. This may involve role-playing exercises, visual aids, or the use of social scripts to enhance their communication abilities.

Social skills encompass a wide range of interpersonal abilities, such as active listening, empathy, teamwork, and conflict resolution. For neurodiverse individuals, navigating social interactions can be particularly daunting. Career coaches must provide targeted support to help these individuals develop the necessary social skills to thrive in the workplace. This may involve providing explicit instruction on social norms, helping them understand unwritten rules, or facilitating social skills groups where they can practice and receive feedback in a safe environment.

In addition to individual coaching, it is crucial to foster a supportive and inclusive environment within organizations. Educators, human resources professionals, and other stakeholders involved in supporting the career development of neurodiverse individuals should collaborate to create an inclusive workplace culture. This can be achieved through awareness training for colleagues, promoting diversity and inclusion initiatives, and offering mentorship programs for neurodiverse employees.

Furthermore, technology can play a vital role in enhancing communication and social skills. Various apps and software programs are available that can provide real-time feedback, assist with social interactions, or facilitate communication. Career coaches should explore these resources and recommend them to neurodiverse individuals as appropriate.

By focusing on communication and social skills development, career coaches can empower neurodiverse individuals to overcome their challenges and succeed in their chosen careers. Through personalized coaching, creating inclusive environments, and leveraging technology, we can ensure that neurodiverse individuals have the tools and support they need to thrive in the workplace.

Executive Functioning

Executive functioning encompasses a set of cognitive processes that aid individuals in planning, organizing, and effectively managing their thoughts, actions, and time. These functions are pivotal in the daily functioning of individuals, particularly in their professional lives. For neurodiverse individuals, who often encounter distinctive challenges in executive functioning, understanding and cultivating these skills become even more crucial.

Within the realm of career coaching and development for neurodiverse individuals, focusing on executive functioning emerges as a critical area. Many neurodiverse individuals grapple with facets like time management, organization, and decision-making, significantly impacting their overall career trajectory. It's imperative for career coaches, educators, human resources professionals, and others supporting neurodiverse individuals to comprehend the specific executive functioning challenges they face and devise strategies to help them surmount these hurdles.

One prevalent executive functioning challenge among neurodiverse individuals revolves around task initiation and organization. Initiating tasks or breaking them down into manageable steps can be challenging. Coaches and educators should offer clear instructions, establish routines, and aid in creating systems for work organization. Breaking tasks into smaller parts can alleviate feelings of overwhelm and enhance productivity.

Another area where executive functioning is often affected in neurodiverse individuals is time management. Challenges may arise in estimating time, task prioritization, and meeting deadlines. Coaches and educators can impart strategies such as visual schedules, setting reminders, and creating structured routines. These techniques aid in developing effective time management skills, ultimately enhancing productivity and reducing stress.

Moreover, decision-making and problem-solving skills hold immense significance for career success. Neurodiverse individuals might face hurdles in these domains due to information processing difficulties or struggles in considering multiple perspectives. Professionals supporting neurodiverse individuals should offer guidance and teach strategies for informed decision-making. This might involve breaking decisions into pros and cons, seeking advice, or utilizing visual aids for information analysis.

In essence, executive functioning significantly influences the career development of neurodiverse individuals. Addressing specific challenges in areas like task initiation, time management, and decision-making empowers career coaches, educators, human resources professionals, and other stakeholders supporting neurodiverse individuals to enhance their executive functioning skills, paving the way for greater success in their careers.

Sensory Sensitivities

Subchapter: Sensory Sensitivities

Introduction:

In the realm of neurodiversity, sensory sensitivities play an integral role in the lives of individuals on the spectrum. Understanding and addressing these sensitivities is essential for career coaches, educators, human resources professionals, and others involved in supporting the career development of neurodiverse individuals. This subchapter delves into the intricacies of sensory sensitivities, providing insights and strategies to empower and enable individuals to thrive in their professional lives.

Understanding Sensory Sensitivities:

Neurodiverse individuals often experience sensory sensitivities, where their sensory systems react differently to stimuli compared to neurotypical individuals. These sensitivities can manifest in various forms, such as hypersensitivity or hyposensitivity to sound, touch, taste, smell, or visual stimuli. Career coaches must recognize the impact of sensory sensitivities on individuals' workplace experiences and take steps to address these challenges.

Creating a Sensory-Inclusive Environment:

To support neurodiverse individuals, it is crucial to create a sensory-inclusive environment in the workplace. This involves making necessary accommodations, such as providing noise-cancelling headphones, adjusting lighting levels, offering flexible workspaces, or implementing sensory breaks. By understanding and addressing sensory sensitivities, career coaches can help individuals feel more comfortable and maximize their potential in the workplace.

Strategies for Sensory Integration:

In this section, we explore various strategies for sensory integration that can assist neurodiverse individuals in effectively managing their sensory sensitivities. These strategies may include sensory diets, which involve incorporating specific sensory activities into daily routines to regulate sensory input. Additionally, we discuss the importance of self-awareness and self-advocacy, empowering individuals to communicate their needs and preferences to colleagues and employers.

Building Resilience and Coping Mechanisms:

Sensory sensitivities can sometimes lead to heightened stress or anxiety in the workplace. Career coaches play a pivotal role in helping neurodiverse individuals build resilience and develop coping mechanisms to navigate these challenges. We outline techniques such as deep breathing exercises, mindfulness practices, and sensory grounding techniques that can assist individuals in managing sensory overload and maintaining their focus and productivity.

Collaboration with Employers:

Finally, this subchapter emphasizes the significance of collaboration between career coaches and employers in accommodating sensory sensitivities. By educating employers about sensory sensitivities and advocating for workplace adjustments, career coaches can foster an environment that supports the diverse needs of neurodiverse individuals. We provide guidance on initiating these conversations and building strong partnerships with employers to ensure long-term success and inclusivity.

Conclusion

Understanding and addressing sensory sensitivities is crucial for career coaches, educators, and human resources professionals focused on supporting the career development of neurodiverse individuals. By creating sensory-inclusive environments, implementing effective strategies for sensory integration, building resilience, and collaborating with employers, career coaches can enable neurodiverse individuals to thrive in their chosen careers, fully embracing their differences and achieving their professional goals.

Anxiety and Stress Management

In the pursuit of career success, individuals with neurodiverse conditions often face unique challenges that can lead to increased anxiety and stress. Understanding and effectively managing these emotions is crucial for their overall well-being and professional growth. This subchapter aims to provide valuable insights and practical strategies for career coaches, educators, human resources professionals, and others involved in supporting the career development of neurodiverse individuals.

Firstly, it is important to recognize that anxiety and stress are common experiences for many neurodiverse individuals. The unique cognitive and sensory processing differences associated with conditions such as autism, ADHD, and dyslexia can often result in heightened levels of anxiety in social, academic, and professional settings. Coaches and support professionals must be empathetic and understanding when addressing these concerns.

One effective strategy is to help individuals identify and understand their specific triggers for anxiety and stress. By recognizing these triggers, individuals can develop personalized coping mechanisms and strategies. Encouraging self-reflection and introspection can empower neurodiverse individuals to take control of their emotional well-being and develop resilience in the face of challenges.

Additionally, coaches should explore various relaxation techniques and stress management strategies that can benefit neurodiverse individuals. These may include mindfulness exercises, deep breathing techniques, and progressive muscle relaxation. Educating individuals about the physiological and psychological impact of stress on their performance and well-being can also be helpful in motivating them to adopt stress management practices.

Support professionals should also consider the environmental factors that contribute to anxiety and stress. Creating a positive and inclusive work or learning environment can significantly reduce stress levels for neurodiverse individuals. This may involve implementing sensory-friendly spaces, providing clear communication channels, and offering accommodations tailored to their unique needs.

Furthermore, coaches should emphasize the importance of self-care and work-life balance. Neurodiverse individuals may be prone to overworking or neglecting their personal well-being due to their drive for success. Teaching them effective time management and boundary-setting skills can help prevent burnout and promote overall mental health.

In conclusion, anxiety and stress management are crucial components of supporting the career development of neurodiverse individuals. By understanding their unique challenges, identifying triggers, promoting relaxation techniques, creating inclusive environments, and emphasizing self-care, coaches and support professionals can empower neurodiverse individuals to overcome anxiety and stress, leading to greater success in their careers.

Benefits of Career Coaching for Neurodiverse Individuals

Career coaching plays a vital role in supporting the career development and success of neurodiverse individuals. By providing tailored guidance and support, career coaches can help these individuals overcome challenges and leverage their unique strengths to achieve their professional goals. In this subchapter, we will explore the numerous benefits of career coaching for neurodiverse individuals.

1. Identifying Strengths and Interests: Career coaching allows neurodiverse individuals to discover their unique strengths, talents, and interests. By understanding their specific skills and abilities, individuals can make informed decisions about their career path and find roles that align with their strengths.
2. Building Self-Confidence: Neurodiverse individuals often face self-doubt and lack of confidence in their abilities.

Career coaching provides a safe and supportive environment where individuals can gain confidence in their skills and capabilities. Coaches focus on empowering individuals, helping them recognize their worth, and fostering a positive mindset.

3. Developing Effective Communication Skills: Effective communication skills are essential in the workplace. Career coaches work closely with neurodiverse individuals to develop and enhance their communication abilities, including verbal and non-verbal communication, active listening, and conflict resolution. These skills help individuals navigate workplace interactions and build positive relationships with colleagues and supervisors.

4. Enhancing Job Search Strategies: Neurodiverse individuals often face unique challenges in finding employment. Career coaches assist in developing effective job search strategies, including resume writing, interview preparation, and networking skills. They provide guidance on how to present strengths and address any potential gaps or challenges during the job application process.

5. Navigating Workplace Accommodations: Many neurodiverse individuals require workplace accommodations to thrive in their roles. Career coaches collaborate with individuals and employers to identify and implement suitable accommodations, ensuring a supportive work environment that promotes productivity and success.

6. Long-Term Career Planning: Career coaching focuses not only on immediate goals but also on long-term career planning. Coaches help neurodiverse individuals set realistic career goals, create action plans, and navigate career transitions. They provide ongoing support and guidance throughout the individual's career journey.

In conclusion, career coaching offers numerous benefits for neurodiverse individuals. By providing tailored support, identifying strengths, building confidence, enhancing communication skills, and assisting in job search strategies and workplace accommodations, career coaches empower neurodiverse individuals to achieve their career goals and lead fulfilling professional lives.

Building a Supportive Relationship with the Coachee

Establishing a supportive and empathetic relationship with the coachee is fundamental in the process of career coaching for neurodiverse individuals. These individuals often face unique challenges and require tailored support to thrive in their professional journeys. In this subchapter, we will explore strategies and techniques to build a strong and supportive relationship with the coachee, ensuring their success and growth.

First and foremost, it is essential for career coaches, educators, human resources professionals, and other individuals involved in supporting neurodiverse individuals to educate themselves about neurodiversity. Understanding the diverse range of neurodivergent conditions and their potential impact on career development is crucial. By acquiring this knowledge, coaches can approach their coachees with sensitivity, empathy, and an open mind.

Active listening is a key skill for building a supportive relationship. Coaches should strive to create a safe and non-judgmental space for the coachee to express their thoughts, concerns, and aspirations. By actively listening, coaches can gain a deeper understanding of the coachee's unique needs, strengths, and challenges, enabling them to provide more targeted and effective support.

Adopting a strength-based approach is another essential aspect of building a supportive relationship. Neurodiverse individuals often possess exceptional talents and abilities that can be harnessed for career success. Coaches should focus on identifying and leveraging these strengths, empowering the coachee to embrace their differences and capitalize on their unique skills.

Establishing clear and open lines of communication is vital to a supportive relationship. Coaches should encourage the coachee to express their thoughts and concerns openly, while also providing regular feedback and guidance. By fostering an environment of open communication, coaches can develop trust and mutual respect with the coachee, enhancing the effectiveness of the coaching process.

Lastly, coaches should strive to create a collaborative partnership with the coachee. By involving the coachee in the decision-making process and jointly setting goals, coaches can ensure that the coaching journey is tailored to the coachee's specific needs and aspirations. This collaborative approach empowers the coachee, instilling a sense of ownership and accountability for their career development.

In conclusion, building a supportive relationship with the coachee is a crucial aspect of career coaching for neurodiverse individuals. By educating themselves, actively listening, adopting a strength-based approach, fostering open communication, and creating a collaborative partnership, coaches can provide the necessary support and guidance for neurodiverse individuals to thrive in their professional journeys.

Setting Realistic Goals and Expectations

When it comes to career coaching and development for neurodiverse individuals, it is crucial to set realistic goals and expectations. Neurodiverse individuals possess unique strengths and abilities, but they may also face specific challenges that can impact their career journey. By understanding these differences and tailoring our approach accordingly, we can empower and support them in achieving success.

One of the first steps in setting realistic goals is to have an open and honest conversation with neurodiverse individuals about their aspirations, interests, and strengths. By actively listening and engaging them in the process, career coaches can gain valuable insights into their goals and desires. It is essential to encourage them to think big but also ensure that their goals are practical and achievable within their individual circumstances.

It is equally important to help neurodiverse individuals develop a comprehensive understanding of their strengths and areas for improvement. By highlighting their unique abilities, coaches can build their confidence and self-esteem. At the same time, coaches should provide constructive feedback to help them address any challenges they may face. This feedback should be delivered in a supportive and empowering manner, focusing on growth rather than limitations.

Another crucial aspect of setting realistic goals is managing expectations. Neurodiverse individuals may face certain obstacles that could impact their career trajectory. It is vital to acknowledge these challenges while emphasizing that they do not define their potential for success. By helping them understand and accept their limitations, coaches can guide them to make informed decisions and set achievable goals that align with their capabilities.

In addition to individual goals, it is essential to set realistic expectations in the broader career context. Coaches should help neurodiverse individuals understand the job market, employment trends, and industry requirements. By providing accurate information, coaches can enable them to make informed choices and set realistic expectations about their career progression.

Ultimately, setting realistic goals and expectations for neurodiverse individuals is about promoting self-awareness, empowerment, and independence. By understanding their unique strengths, challenges, and limitations, coaches can help them navigate their career paths with confidence and resilience. Through ongoing support and guidance, neurodiverse individuals can achieve their goals and find fulfillment in their chosen careers.

CHAPTER 3

Creating a Neurodiverse-Friendly Workplace

Educating Employers on Neurodiversity

Subchapter: Educating Employers on Neurodiversity

In today's rapidly evolving workplace, it is essential for employers to understand and embrace neurodiversity. Neurodiverse individuals bring unique perspectives, talents, and skills to the table, making them valuable assets to any organization. However, many employers are still unaware of what neurodiversity entails and how to effectively support and integrate these individuals into their workforce.

This subchapter aims to educate employers on the importance of neurodiversity and provide guidance on creating an inclusive and supportive work environment for neurodiverse individuals. By understanding the benefits of neurodiversity and implementing appropriate strategies, employers can tap into a pool of diverse talent and foster a culture of inclusion and innovation.

The journey towards educating employers on neurodiversity begins with dispelling common misconceptions. Many employers may have preconceived notions about neurodiverse individuals, such as their inability to work effectively in a team or their limited problem-solving skills. It is crucial to challenge these stereotypes and provide accurate information about the strengths and abilities of neurodiverse individuals.

One effective way to educate employers is by highlighting successful case studies and real-life examples. Showcasing individuals who have excelled in their careers despite their neurodiverse traits can help employers understand that neurodiversity is not a barrier to success but rather an opportunity for growth and innovation. These stories can serve as powerful testimonials that inspire employers to rethink their hiring practices and create a more inclusive workplace.

Additionally, providing employers with practical strategies and resources can help them better support neurodiverse employees. This subchapter will explore various accommodations and adjustments that can be made in the workplace, such as flexible work arrangements, clear communication channels, and tailored training programs. Employers will also learn about the importance of fostering a culture of acceptance and understanding, where neurodiverse individuals feel valued and empowered to contribute their unique perspectives.

By educating employers on neurodiversity, we can bridge the gap between talent and opportunity. With the right knowledge and tools, employers can create a work environment that celebrates diversity and unlocks the full potential of neurodiverse individuals. Embracing neurodiversity not only benefits the individual but also leads to increased productivity, enhanced creativity, and a more inclusive and equitable society.

Addressing Stigma and Prejudice

In the journey towards creating a more inclusive and diverse society, it is vital to address the stigma and prejudice that neurodiverse individuals often face. The subchapter "Addressing Stigma and Prejudice" in our book, "Embracing Differences: Career Coaching for Neurodiverse Individuals," aims to shed light on this important topic and provide strategies to combat these challenges.

Neurodiverse individuals, including those with autism, ADHD, dyslexia, and other neurological differences, often encounter societal biases that hinder their career development and success. The stigma associated with these conditions can lead to prejudice, discrimination, and exclusion in various professional settings. As career coaches, educators, and HR professionals, it is our responsibility to understand and address these issues to create a more inclusive and supportive environment for neurodiverse individuals.

This subchapter delves into the root causes of stigma and prejudice towards neurodiversity, exploring societal misconceptions and stereotypes that contribute to these biases. By understanding the origins of stigma, we can effectively challenge and debunk common misconceptions and promote a more accurate understanding of neurodiversity.

Furthermore, we provide practical strategies and tools to help career coaches and professionals address stigma and prejudice in their work. These strategies include promoting education and awareness about neurodiversity, fostering empathy and understanding among colleagues and employers, and advocating for inclusive workplace policies and practices. By implementing these strategies, we can create inclusive environments that celebrate the strengths and unique contributions of neurodiverse individuals.

Additionally, the subchapter highlights the importance of self-advocacy for neurodiverse individuals. Empowering them to speak up about their needs, strengths, and aspirations can help combat stigma and prejudice. By equipping neurodiverse individuals with self-advocacy skills, we can support their journey towards achieving career success and independence.

In conclusion, addressing stigma and prejudice is crucial in creating a more inclusive and supportive environment for neurodiverse individuals. This subchapter provides valuable insights, strategies, and tools to help career coaches, educators, HR professionals, and others involved in supporting the career development of neurodiverse individuals navigate these challenges. By embracing differences and fostering a culture of acceptance and understanding, we can pave the way for a more inclusive and successful future for all.

Providing Reasonable Accommodations

In the pursuit of creating inclusive and diverse workplaces, it is essential for career coaches, educators, human resources professionals, and others involved in supporting the career development of neurodiverse individuals to understand the importance of providing reasonable accommodations. By offering these accommodations, employers can create an environment that empowers and enables neurodiverse individuals to thrive in their careers.

Reasonable accommodations are modifications or adjustments made to a job or work environment to ensure that individuals with neurodiverse conditions can perform their duties effectively. These accommodations are tailored to meet the specific needs of each individual and can range from changes in workplace policies and procedures to modifications in physical workspaces.

One of the key benefits of providing reasonable accommodations is the ability to level the playing field for neurodiverse individuals. By identifying and addressing barriers that may hinder their success, these accommodations enable them to showcase their unique talents and abilities. For example, individuals with autism spectrum disorder may excel in tasks that require attention to detail and pattern recognition. By providing a quiet workspace with minimal sensory distractions, employers can create an environment conducive to their optimal performance.

Another crucial aspect of providing reasonable accommodations is fostering open communication between employers and neurodiverse individuals. It is essential to create a safe and supportive environment where individuals feel comfortable disclosing their neurodiverse conditions and discussing their specific needs. This dialogue allows employers to better understand the challenges these individuals face and identify appropriate accommodations to address them effectively.

Furthermore, reasonable accommodations not only benefit individuals with neurodiverse conditions but also contribute to the overall success and productivity of the organization. Research has shown that companies that embrace diversity and provide accommodations have higher employee satisfaction, increased retention rates, and improved innovation and problem-solving capabilities.

In conclusion, the provision of reasonable accommodations is an essential component of supporting the career development of neurodiverse individuals. Career coaches, educators, human resources professionals, and others involved in this process play a pivotal role in advocating for and facilitating these accommodations. By creating an inclusive and accommodating work environment, we can empower neurodiverse individuals to reach their full potential, contribute meaningfully to their organizations, and ensure a more diverse and inclusive workforce.

Promoting Inclusion and Diversity

In today's rapidly evolving world, fostering inclusion and diversity has become a crucial aspect of any organization or institution. This subchapter aims to provide valuable insights and practical strategies for career coaches, educators, human resources professionals, and others involved in supporting the career development of neurodiverse individuals, with a primary focus on promoting inclusion and diversity.

Understanding the concept of neurodiversity is the first step towards creating an inclusive and diverse environment. Neurodiversity recognizes and appreciates the natural variations in the human brain and the unique strengths and abilities that individuals with diverse neurological profiles bring to the table. By embracing neurodiversity, organizations can tap into a pool of untapped talent and foster a culture of inclusivity.

One effective approach to promoting inclusion and diversity is to implement inclusive hiring practices. This involves creating job descriptions and interview processes that are accommodating to the different needs and abilities of neurodiverse individuals. By providing clear communication and reasonable accommodations during the recruitment process, organizations can ensure that individuals with diverse neurodiverse profiles have an equal opportunity to showcase their skills and abilities.

Furthermore, it is important to provide ongoing support and professional development opportunities for neurodiverse individuals in the workplace. This can include mentoring programs, coaching sessions, and training workshops that focus on building communication skills, social interactions, and self-advocacy. By investing in the development of neurodiverse employees, organizations can create an inclusive and supportive environment that nurtures their talents and helps them thrive in their careers.

Additionally, organizations can foster inclusion and diversity by promoting awareness and understanding among all employees. This can be achieved through diversity training programs, workshops, and awareness campaigns that aim to educate employees about neurodiversity and the unique challenges faced by neurodiverse individuals. By fostering a culture of empathy, respect, and acceptance, organizations can create an environment where everyone feels valued and supported.

In conclusion, promoting inclusion and diversity is essential for the career success of neurodiverse individuals. By embracing neurodiversity, implementing inclusive hiring practices, providing ongoing support, and promoting awareness, organizations can create a workplace that celebrates differences and harnesses the strengths of all individuals. By adopting these strategies, career coaches, educators, human resources professionals, and other stakeholders can play a pivotal role in empowering neurodiverse individuals and helping them achieve their full potential in their chosen careers.

Creating Supportive Work Environments

In the journey to empower and maximize the potential of neurodiverse individuals, creating supportive work environments is critical for their career success. A supportive work environment not only benefits the neurodiverse individuals but also fosters a culture of inclusion and diversity within the organization. In this subchapter, we will explore key strategies and practices that career coaches, educators, human resources professionals, and others involved in supporting the career development of neurodiverse individuals can implement to create such environments.

One of the fundamental aspects of creating a supportive work environment is raising awareness and understanding about neurodiversity. Educating employers, colleagues, and teams about the unique strengths and challenges of neurodiverse individuals helps to break down stereotypes and misconceptions. By promoting empathy and acceptance, organizations can lay the foundation for an inclusive workplace culture.

Another crucial element is providing reasonable accommodations. Neurodiverse individuals may require specific accommodations to perform at their best. Career coaches can work closely with employers to identify and implement these accommodations, such as flexible work hours, noise-canceling headphones, or visual aids. By tailoring the work environment to the individual's needs, employers can create a level playing field for all employees, fostering a sense of belonging and equal opportunity.

Communication and social skills training are also essential components of creating supportive work environments. Career coaches can help neurodiverse individuals develop effective communication techniques and interpersonal skills that enable them to navigate workplace interactions more successfully. By providing specific guidance and practice, individuals can enhance their ability to collaborate, resolve conflicts, and build relationships, ultimately contributing to a more harmonious and productive work environment.

Additionally, fostering mentorship and peer support programs can greatly benefit neurodiverse individuals. Having a mentor or a support network within the organization can provide valuable guidance, encouragement, and a sense of belonging. Career coaches can play a vital role in connecting individuals with suitable mentors and facilitating the establishment of peer support networks.

Finally, implementing a culture of appreciation and recognition is essential. Recognizing and celebrating the unique contributions that neurodiverse individuals bring to the workplace not only boosts their confidence but also creates an inclusive atmosphere that values diversity. Career coaches can work with organizations to develop recognition programs that highlight the achievements and strengths of neurodiverse individuals, reinforcing their sense of worth and value within the organization.

Creating supportive work environments for neurodiverse individuals is an ongoing process that requires collaboration, understanding, and commitment from all stakeholders. By implementing these strategies and practices, career coaches, educators, human resources professionals, and others involved in supporting the career development of neurodiverse individuals can make a significant impact on their journey towards empowerment and independence.

CHAPTER 4

Assessing and Developing Skills for Career Success

Identifying Strengths and Interests

In the journey towards career success for neurodiverse individuals, it is crucial to begin by identifying their unique strengths and interests. By understanding and leveraging these qualities, career coaches, educators, human resources professionals, and others involved in supporting the career development of neurodiverse individuals can empower them to flourish in their chosen paths.

Neurodiverse individuals possess a wide range of strengths that contribute to their success in the workplace. These strengths may include exceptional attention to detail, pattern recognition, creativity, problem-solving abilities, and a strong focus on tasks. By recognizing and harnessing these strengths, career coaches can guide neurodiverse individuals towards careers that align with their natural abilities, increasing the likelihood of job satisfaction and success.

One effective way to identify strengths and interests is through comprehensive assessments and evaluations. These assessments can provide valuable insights into an individual's cognitive abilities, personality traits, and occupational preferences. By administering these assessments, career coaches can gain a deeper understanding of the neurodiverse individual's unique profile and tailor their career guidance accordingly.

In addition to formal assessments, career coaches should engage in open and honest conversations with neurodiverse individuals to explore their interests, passions, and goals. By actively listening and providing a safe and supportive environment, coaches can encourage self-reflection and help individuals recognize their true potential. Through this exploration, individuals may discover unexpected strengths and uncover previously unrecognized talents.

Furthermore, it is essential to consider the individual's specific neurodivergent condition when identifying strengths and interests. Each condition, whether autism spectrum disorder, ADHD, dyslexia, or others, presents its own unique set of strengths and challenges. By understanding the specific traits associated with a particular condition, career coaches can provide more tailored guidance and support, ensuring that the individual's strengths are maximized and their challenges are accommodated.

Lastly, it is important to approach the identification of strengths and interests with a growth mindset. Encouraging neurodiverse individuals to embrace their strengths while also challenging themselves to develop new skills fosters personal and professional growth. By continuously expanding their abilities, individuals can adapt to changing career landscapes and seize new opportunities.

In conclusion, identifying strengths and interests is a fundamental step in coaching neurodiverse individuals towards career success. By recognizing and leveraging their unique qualities, career coaches can empower neurodiverse individuals to pursue meaningful careers that align with their natural abilities. Through comprehensive assessments, open conversations, an understanding of their specific neurodivergent condition, and a growth mindset, coaches can provide tailored guidance and support, ensuring long-term career satisfaction and independence.

Enhancing Communication and Social Skills

In the constantly evolving professional landscape, effective communication and strong social skills have become essential for career success. However, for neurodiverse individuals, navigating the nuances of social interaction and communication can pose significant challenges. This subchapter aims to provide valuable insights and strategies to enhance communication and social skills, specifically tailored for neurodiverse individuals, empowering them to thrive in their careers.

Understanding the unique communication styles and preferences of neurodiverse individuals is crucial. Career coaches, educators, and HR professionals must recognize that neurodiverse individuals may process information differently, interpret social cues uniquely, and express themselves in distinct ways. By acknowledging these differences and adopting a flexible, inclusive approach, professionals can ensure effective communication and foster a positive, inclusive work environment.

One key strategy for enhancing communication skills in neurodiverse individuals is providing clear and explicit instructions. Breaking down complex tasks into smaller, manageable steps and using visual aids or written instructions can greatly facilitate understanding and reduce anxiety. Additionally, utilizing technology tools, such as communication apps or assistive devices, can bridge communication gaps and empower individuals to express their thoughts and ideas more effectively.

Another vital aspect of enhancing social skills is nurturing self-awareness and emotional intelligence. By encouraging neurodiverse individuals to recognize and understand their emotions and reactions, professionals can help them develop effective coping mechanisms and navigate social interactions better. Implementing social skills training programs and incorporating role-playing exercises can provide practical opportunities to practice and refine social skills in a safe, supportive environment.

Moreover, promoting inclusive workplaces that embrace diversity and encourage open communication is crucial. Establishing mentorship programs and peer support networks fosters connections and provides neurodiverse individuals with opportunities to learn from colleagues, gaining valuable social skills through observation and guidance.

In conclusion, enhancing communication and social skills is essential to empower neurodiverse individuals in their career development. Understanding their unique communication styles, providing clear instructions, nurturing self-awareness, and fostering inclusive work environments will enable career coaches, educators, and HR professionals to play a pivotal role in helping neurodiverse individuals thrive in their professional lives. Embracing differences and offering tailored support benefits not only neurodiverse individuals but also contributes to creating diverse, inclusive, and successful workplaces for everyone.

Improving Executive Functioning Skills

Executive functioning skills are a set of cognitive processes that enable individuals to plan, organize, manage time, and regulate their behavior effectively. For neurodiverse individuals, who may experience challenges in these areas, developing and enhancing executive functioning skills is crucial for achieving career success. This subchapter explores various strategies and techniques to improve executive functioning skills and empower neurodiverse individuals to thrive in their careers.

One of the key aspects of improving executive functioning skills is enhancing self-awareness. Neurodiverse individuals need to understand their strengths and weaknesses in areas such as time management, organization, task initiation, and impulse control. By recognizing their specific challenges, they can tailor strategies and accommodations to address these areas effectively.

Another important aspect is developing effective planning and organization skills. Neurodiverse individuals can benefit from using visual tools, such as calendars, to break down tasks and deadlines into smaller, manageable steps. Additionally, creating to-do lists, prioritizing tasks, and utilizing reminders can help in staying focused and on track.

Time management is another critical skill to develop. Neurodiverse individuals may struggle with estimating time accurately and staying on schedule. Using timers, setting realistic goals, and breaking tasks into smaller time blocks can be useful strategies to overcome these challenges.

Furthermore, building strategies to improve attention and focus is essential. Techniques like chunking information, using visual aids, and minimizing distractions can aid in maintaining concentration and completing tasks efficiently.

Additionally, regulating emotions and managing stress are crucial for executive functioning. Neurodiverse individuals can benefit from learning relaxation techniques, such as deep breathing and mindfulness, to reduce anxiety and maintain emotional stability. Seeking support from mentors, coaches, or therapists can also help in developing effective coping strategies.

Finally, fostering self-advocacy skills is vital for neurodiverse individuals to succeed in their careers. By understanding their strengths, challenges, and the accommodations they require, they can confidently communicate their needs to employers and colleagues. This can help create an inclusive work environment that accommodates their unique neurodiverse traits.

In conclusion, improving executive functioning skills is essential for the career success of neurodiverse individuals. By enhancing self-awareness, developing planning and organization skills, managing time effectively, improving attention and focus, regulating emotions, and fostering self-advocacy, neurodiverse individuals can overcome challenges and thrive in their chosen careers. Career coaches, educators, human resources professionals, and others involved in supporting the career development of neurodiverse individuals can utilize these strategies to empower and guide their clients towards achieving their professional goals.

Managing Sensory Sensitivities in the Workplace

Sensory sensitivities can significantly impact the daily lives of neurodiverse individuals, including their experiences in the workplace. As career coaches, educators, human resources professionals, and others involved in supporting the career development of neurodiverse individuals, it is essential to understand the challenges they face and provide strategies to manage sensory sensitivities effectively.

Sensory sensitivities can manifest in various ways, such as hypersensitivity to noise, touch, light, or smells. These sensitivities can lead to sensory overload, anxiety, and reduced productivity in the workplace. However, with the right guidance and support, individuals with sensory sensitivities can thrive in their careers.

One crucial step in managing sensory sensitivities is creating a sensory-friendly work environment. This can involve making small adjustments like providing noise-cancelling headphones, offering flexible lighting options, or allocating quiet spaces where employees can take breaks when needed. By implementing these accommodations, employers can create an inclusive environment that supports the needs of neurodiverse individuals.

Another essential aspect of managing sensory sensitivities is communication. Open and honest dialogue between the individual and their employer, colleagues, and support network is crucial. Encouraging neurodiverse individuals to share their specific sensory sensitivities and triggers can facilitate understanding and empathy from those around them. Employers should also be receptive to feedback and make necessary adjustments to ensure the work environment is conducive to the individual's success.

Additionally, implementing sensory breaks throughout the workday can be highly beneficial. These breaks allow individuals to recharge and regulate their sensory systems, reducing the risk of overload. Career coaches can work with neurodiverse individuals to identify personalized sensory strategies, such as deep breathing exercises, stretching, or engaging in calming activities during these breaks.

Finally, it is crucial to educate employers and colleagues about neurodiversity and sensory sensitivities. By raising awareness and promoting acceptance, organizations can foster a culture of understanding and support. Training programs, workshops, and informational resources can help dispel misconceptions and enable colleagues to provide the necessary support and accommodations.

Managing sensory sensitivities in the workplace is a collaborative effort that requires the involvement of career coaches, educators, human resources professionals, and others committed to supporting neurodiverse individuals. By prioritizing sensory-friendly environments, open communication, sensory breaks, and education, we can empower neurodiverse individuals to thrive in their careers and create a more inclusive and diverse workforce.

Coping Strategies for Anxiety and Stress

When it comes to supporting the career development of neurodiverse individuals, it is important to address the unique challenges they may face, such as anxiety and stress. In this subchapter, we will explore effective coping strategies that can help individuals navigate these difficulties and thrive in their professional lives.

1. Mindfulness and Relaxation Techniques: One powerful strategy for managing anxiety and stress is practicing mindfulness. Encouraging neurodiverse individuals to engage in mindfulness exercises, such as deep breathing or meditation, can help them become more aware of their emotions and create a sense of calm. Relaxation techniques, such as progressive muscle relaxation or guided imagery, can also be beneficial in reducing stress levels.

2. Self-Care and Healthy Habits: It is crucial for neurodiverse individuals to prioritize self-care and develop healthy habits. This includes getting enough sleep, eating nutritious meals, and engaging in regular physical activity. When individuals take care of their physical well-being, they are better equipped to manage stress and anxiety.

3. Time Management and Organization: Neurodiverse individuals often benefit from structure and routine. Helping them develop effective time management skills and organizational strategies can alleviate stress and reduce anxiety. Encouraging the use of calendars, to-do lists, and prioritization techniques can assist in managing workload and deadlines.

4. Cognitive Behavioral Techniques: Cognitive Behavioral Therapy (CBT) can be a valuable tool for neurodiverse individuals in managing anxiety and stress. This approach helps individuals identify and challenge negative thought patterns and replace them with more positive and realistic ones. Career coaches can provide guidance on implementing CBT techniques, such as cognitive restructuring and thought stopping.

5. Social Support and Communication Skills: Building a strong support system is essential for neurodiverse individuals. Encourage them to seek out social connections, both within and outside of the workplace. Developing effective communication skills can also help in expressing needs and concerns, reducing stress caused by misunderstandings or conflicts.

6. Seeking Professional Help: It is essential to recognize that some individuals may require professional assistance in managing anxiety and stress. Career coaches should be prepared to refer neurodiverse individuals to mental health professionals who specialize in working with this population. Collaborating with these professionals can provide individuals with the necessary tools and support to overcome their challenges.

By incorporating these coping strategies into their daily lives, neurodiverse individuals can effectively manage anxiety and stress, allowing them to excel in their careers. As career coaches, educators, and human resources professionals, it is our responsibility to provide the necessary resources and support to help neurodiverse individuals thrive professionally.

CHAPTER 5

Effective Job Search Strategies

Resume and Cover Letter Writing Tips

In the competitive job market, creating a compelling resume and cover letter is essential for neurodiverse individuals seeking career success. These documents serve as the first impression for potential employers and can significantly impact job prospects. This subchapter will provide valuable tips and strategies for crafting effective resumes and cover letters tailored to the unique needs of neurodiverse individuals.

1. Understand the Purpose: Begin by explaining to neurodiverse individuals the purpose of a resume and cover letter. Emphasize that these documents are marketing tools that highlight their skills, experiences, and qualifications relevant to the job they are applying for.

2. Structure and Format: Guide individuals on how to structure their resumes and cover letters. Break down the sections to include contact information, objective statement, education, work experience, skills, and references. Recommend using a clean and easy-to-read format, with bullet points and headings for better organization.

3. Highlight Strengths and Accomplishments: Encourage neurodiverse individuals to focus on their strengths and accomplishments when presenting their qualifications. Assist them in identifying their transferable skills and showcasing them effectively to potential employers.

4. Tailor for Each Job Application: Stress the importance of tailoring resumes and cover letters for each job application. Teach individuals to carefully review job descriptions and customize their documents to match the specific requirements and keywords sought by employers.
5. Clear and Concise Language: Help neurodiverse individuals communicate their skills and experiences clearly and concisely. Suggest using action verbs, avoiding jargon, and using simple language that can be easily understood by employers.
6. Seek Proofreading and Feedback: Encourage individuals to seek assistance from career coaches, educators, or trusted individuals for proofreading and feedback on their resumes and cover letters. This will help identify any errors, improve clarity, and ensure that the documents effectively represent their unique strengths.
7. Addressing Employment Gaps: Guide neurodiverse individuals on how to effectively address employment gaps in their resumes. Help them focus on any relevant activities, volunteer work, or training they may have undertaken during those periods.
8. Create a Strong Cover Letter: Teach individuals how to craft a compelling cover letter that complements their resume. Explain that the cover letter should briefly introduce themselves, express their interest in the position, and highlight key qualifications and experiences that make them an ideal candidate.

By providing these resume and cover letter writing tips, career coaches, educators, and human resources professionals can empower and support neurodiverse individuals on their journey towards career success. Tailoring these documents to highlight their strengths and unique abilities will increase their chances of securing meaningful employment opportunities.

Networking for Neurodiverse Individuals

Networking plays a crucial role in career success for individuals of all backgrounds and abilities. However, for neurodiverse individuals, navigating social interactions and building connections can present unique challenges. In this subchapter, we will explore strategies and techniques specifically tailored to help neurodiverse individuals effectively network and build meaningful professional relationships.

Understanding the challenges faced by neurodiverse individuals in networking is essential for career coaches, educators, human resources professionals, and others involved in supporting their career development. Sensory sensitivities, difficulties with social cues and communication, and anxiety can all impact their ability to network confidently and authentically.

To begin, it is important to create a safe and inclusive environment for neurodiverse individuals to practice and refine their networking skills. This can be achieved through role-playing exercises, mock networking events, and providing clear and concise instructions on how to initiate and maintain conversations. By offering a structured and supportive environment, coaches and educators can help neurodiverse individuals build their confidence and ease anxiety associated with networking.

Additionally, understanding and leveraging the strengths of neurodiverse individuals can be a valuable asset in networking situations. Many neurodiverse individuals possess exceptional attention to detail, deep knowledge in specific areas of interest, and strong problem-solving skills. Coaches and professionals should encourage them to highlight these strengths when engaging with others in a professional setting, as it can make a lasting impression and open doors for further opportunities.

Furthermore, incorporating technology and online platforms into networking strategies can be particularly beneficial for neurodiverse individuals. Virtual networking events, social media platforms, and professional networking websites allow for controlled interactions and give individuals the opportunity to showcase their skills and expertise without the pressure of face-to-face interactions. Educators and coaches should guide neurodiverse individuals on how to effectively utilize these tools to expand their network and connect with professionals in their desired fields.

Lastly, it is vital to address the importance of self-advocacy and disclosure in networking. Neurodiverse individuals should be encouraged to communicate their unique needs and strengths to potential networking contacts. This transparency not only helps in building authentic relationships but also allows others to understand and appreciate the value neurodiverse individuals can bring to the table.

In conclusion, networking is a critical component of career success for neurodiverse individuals, and tailored strategies can significantly enhance their networking abilities. By creating supportive environments, leveraging their strengths, incorporating technology, and promoting self-advocacy, career coaches, educators, and human resources professionals can empower neurodiverse individuals to navigate networking challenges with confidence and build a strong professional network to support their career development.

Interview Preparation and Techniques

Interviews can be nerve-wracking for anyone, but for neurodiverse individuals, they can be particularly challenging. However, with the right preparation and techniques, anyone can navigate interviews successfully. In this subchapter, we will discuss effective strategies to help neurodiverse individuals prepare for and excel in interviews.

1. Understanding the Interview Process: It is crucial for career coaches, educators, and human resources professionals to familiarize neurodiverse individuals with the interview process. Explaining the different stages, from initial screening to final interview, can help alleviate anxiety and set realistic expectations.

2. Research and Preparation: Encourage neurodiverse individuals to research the company and position they are applying for. This includes understanding the company's values, culture, and recent achievements. Knowledge of the company will not only demonstrate genuine interest but also help in formulating relevant questions.

3. Mock Interviews: Conducting mock interviews is an excellent way to prepare neurodiverse individuals for the real thing. Simulating different interview scenarios will help them become comfortable with answering common questions, maintaining eye contact, and projecting confidence.

4. Communication Strategies: It is essential to work on effective communication skills with neurodiverse individuals. This includes practicing clear and concise responses, active listening, and maintaining appropriate body language. Role-playing exercises can be beneficial in honing these skills.

5. Managing Anxiety: Many neurodiverse individuals experience heightened anxiety during interviews. Encourage them to practice relaxation techniques such as deep breathing and positive visualization. Additionally, remind them to take breaks, engage in self-care activities, and get enough rest before the interview.

6. Disclosing Neurodiversity: Discuss the pros and cons of disclosing neurodiversity during interviews. While some individuals may benefit from disclosing to request reasonable accommodations, others may choose to disclose

only after receiving an offer. Educate neurodiverse individuals on their rights and options.

7. Providing Accommodations: Career coaches and human resources professionals should collaborate to ensure appropriate accommodations are provided during interviews. These may include extended time, written instructions, or a quiet space. Being inclusive and accommodating can create a more equitable and supportive interview environment.

8. Reflecting and Learning: After each interview, encourage neurodiverse individuals to reflect on their performance. Identify areas of improvement and provide constructive feedback. This reflection process will help them grow and develop their interview skills over time.

By focusing on interview preparation and techniques specifically tailored to neurodiverse individuals, career coaches, educators, and human resources professionals can empower them to navigate the interview process with confidence and success. With the right support and strategies in place, neurodiverse individuals can showcase their unique strengths and abilities, ultimately leading to fulfilling and successful careers.

Disclosure and Self-Advocacy

In the journey towards career success, one of the key challenges faced by neurodiverse individuals is deciding whether to disclose their condition and how to effectively self-advocate in the workplace. The subchapter on "Disclosure and Self-Advocacy" in the book "Embracing Differences: Career Coaching for Neurodiverse Individuals" aims to provide valuable insights and strategies to help career coaches, educators, human resources professionals, and others involved in supporting the career development of neurodiverse individuals navigate this complex issue.

Disclosing one's neurodiversity in the workplace is a deeply personal decision. Some individuals may choose to disclose their condition to their employers, while others may prefer to keep it confidential. This subchapter emphasizes the importance of empowering neurodiverse individuals to make informed decisions regarding disclosure. It explores the potential benefits and risks of disclosure, offering guidance on how to assess the workplace culture, evaluate potential accommodations, and anticipate the impact of disclosure on career advancement.

Furthermore, the subchapter delves into the concept of self-advocacy, which plays a crucial role in ensuring success for neurodiverse individuals. It provides practical strategies to help individuals effectively communicate their needs, advocate for accommodations, and seek support from colleagues and supervisors. The subchapter also emphasizes the importance of building self-confidence and developing self-advocacy skills through role-playing exercises, assertiveness training, and the cultivation of a positive self-image.

In addition to the individual level, the subchapter recognizes the role of career coaches, educators, and human resources professionals in supporting neurodiverse individuals in their disclosure and self-advocacy journeys. It offers guidance on creating a safe and inclusive environment, fostering open communication channels, and providing resources and training to enhance the skills of both the individuals and the professionals supporting them.

Ultimately, "Disclosure and Self-Advocacy" is a subchapter that aims to equip the target audience with the knowledge and tools needed to empower neurodiverse individuals in their career development. By understanding the complexities of disclosure and self-advocacy, and by implementing effective strategies, career coaches, educators, human resources professionals, and others involved in supporting neurodiverse individuals can help create a more inclusive and accommodating work environment where everyone can thrive and succeed.

Navigating Online Job Platforms

In today's digital age, online job platforms have become a crucial tool for individuals seeking employment opportunities. This is especially true for neurodiverse individuals who may face unique challenges in their job search. Navigating these platforms effectively requires a deep understanding of their features and functionalities, as well as strategies tailored to the specific needs of neurodiverse job seekers.

The first step in navigating online job platforms is to familiarize oneself with the various platforms available. The most popular platforms include LinkedIn, Indeed, Monster, and Glassdoor. Each platform has its own set of features, such as job alerts, resume builders, and networking capabilities. It is important for career coaches, educators, and HR professionals to be well-versed in these features to guide neurodiverse individuals in maximizing their job search efforts.

One key aspect of online job platforms is the ability to create a compelling and professional online profile. Career coaches can provide guidance on how to optimize profiles to showcase neurodiverse individuals' unique strengths and skills. This may involve highlighting specific accomplishments, certifications, or projects that demonstrate their abilities. Additionally, coaches can help neurodiverse individuals craft an effective personal statement or summary that accurately represents their career goals and aspirations.

Another important consideration when navigating online job platforms is the use of keywords. Many employers use applicant tracking systems (ATS) to scan resumes and profiles for specific keywords related to job requirements. Career coaches can assist neurodiverse individuals in identifying relevant keywords and incorporating them into their resumes and profiles. This increases the likelihood of their profiles being noticed by employers and enhances their chances of securing interviews.

Networking is another crucial aspect of online job platforms. Coaches can guide neurodiverse individuals in building and maintaining professional connections through platforms like LinkedIn. They can provide tips on engaging with others, joining relevant groups, and participating in industry discussions. Effective networking can lead to job referrals, mentorship opportunities, and valuable insights into the job market.

Lastly, it is important for career coaches, educators, and HR professionals to stay updated on the latest trends and developments in online job platforms. These platforms are constantly evolving, and new features are introduced regularly. By staying informed, professionals can provide the most up-to-date guidance to neurodiverse individuals, ensuring they have the knowledge and tools necessary to navigate these platforms successfully.

In conclusion, navigating online job platforms is a critical skill for neurodiverse individuals seeking career success. Career coaches, educators, and HR professionals play a vital role in helping these individuals understand and utilize these platforms effectively. By familiarizing themselves with the features, optimizing profiles, incorporating keywords, and leveraging networking opportunities, neurodiverse individuals can maximize their chances of finding meaningful employment through online job platforms.

CHAPTER 6

Career Development and Advancement

Setting Long-Term Career Goals

One of the most important aspects of career development for neurodiverse individuals is setting long-term career goals. These goals provide a sense of direction, purpose, and motivation, and can help individuals navigate the complexities of the job market. In this subchapter, we will explore the importance of setting long-term career goals and provide practical strategies for helping neurodiverse individuals in their goal-setting process.

Understanding the unique strengths and challenges of neurodiverse individuals is crucial when supporting their career development. By acknowledging their unique abilities, career coaches, educators, and human resources professionals can help these individuals set achievable, yet aspirational, long-term career goals. These goals should align with their passions, interests, and strengths, while also considering their challenges and any necessary accommodations.

To begin the goal-setting process, it is important to encourage neurodiverse individuals to reflect on their personal and professional aspirations. This self-reflection can help them identify their core values, interests, and skills. By gaining a deeper understanding of themselves, they can then align their long-term career goals with their authentic selves.

When setting long-term career goals, it is crucial to break them down into smaller, manageable steps. Neurodiverse individuals may face challenges in planning and executing tasks, so breaking down goals into smaller milestones can make them more achievable and less overwhelming. These milestones can serve as checkpoints along the way, providing a sense of progress and motivation.

Additionally, it is important to encourage neurodiverse individuals to seek support and resources to help them achieve their long-term career goals. This support can come from career coaches, mentors, support groups, or online communities. By creating a network of support, individuals can gain valuable insights, advice, and encouragement throughout their career journey.

Finally, it is essential to regularly review and reassess long-term career goals. As individuals grow, change, and gain new experiences, their goals may evolve. By regularly reviewing and adjusting their goals, neurodiverse individuals can ensure that their career trajectory remains aligned with their changing needs and aspirations.

In conclusion, setting long-term career goals is a crucial step in the career development of neurodiverse individuals. By acknowledging their unique abilities, breaking down goals into manageable steps, seeking support, and regularly reviewing and adjusting goals, these individuals can create a path towards a fulfilling and successful career. As career coaches, educators, and human resources professionals, it is our responsibility to provide the necessary guidance and support to empower neurodiverse individuals in achieving their long-term career goals.

Building Professional Networks

One of the key aspects of career development for neurodiverse individuals is the establishment and cultivation of professional networks. Building professional networks can have a significant impact on their career success and advancement. This subchapter aims to provide insights and strategies for career coaches, educators, human resources professionals, and others involved in supporting the career development of neurodiverse individuals on how to assist their clients in building professional networks.

Neurodiverse individuals often face unique challenges when it comes to networking due to their different communication styles, social anxieties, and difficulties in navigating social interactions. However, with the right guidance and support, they can develop effective networking skills that can open doors to new opportunities and connections.

The subchapter begins by emphasizing the importance of networking and highlighting its benefits for neurodiverse individuals. It emphasizes that networking is not just about seeking job opportunities but also about building relationships, gaining knowledge, and accessing support and resources.

Next, the subchapter delves into practical strategies and techniques for networking. It provides step-by-step guidance on how to identify potential networking opportunities, how to approach and engage with others, and how to maintain and nurture professional relationships over time. It also discusses the effective use of online platforms and social media for networking purposes.

Additionally, the subchapter acknowledges the specific challenges that neurodiverse individuals may face in networking situations and offers advice on how to overcome them. It provides tips on managing social anxieties, navigating small talk, and building connections based on shared interests and strengths.

Furthermore, the subchapter discusses the importance of mentorship and sponsorship in the career development of neurodiverse individuals. It explores how career coaches and other professionals can help facilitate mentorship relationships and advocate for their clients within their professional networks.

Overall, this subchapter aims to equip career coaches, educators, human resources professionals, and others involved in supporting the career development of neurodiverse individuals with practical strategies and insights for helping their clients build professional networks. By empowering neurodiverse individuals with networking skills, they can increase their chances of career success and create a sense of empowerment and independence in their professional lives.

Seeking Mentors and Role Models

One crucial aspect of career coaching and development for neurodiverse individuals is the importance of seeking mentors and role models. Mentors and role models can provide invaluable guidance, support, and inspiration to those navigating their career paths, particularly for individuals who may face unique challenges due to their neurodiversity. In this subchapter, we will explore the significance of seeking mentors and role models and provide practical strategies for finding and cultivating these relationships.

Mentors and role models can serve as beacons of hope and success for neurodiverse individuals. They offer personal insights, share their own experiences, and provide guidance on overcoming obstacles in the workplace. By connecting with someone who has successfully navigated the challenges of their own neurodiversity, individuals can gain confidence and learn valuable strategies for achieving career success. Mentors and role models can also offer a source of inspiration, showing what is possible and motivating individuals to pursue their goals.

Finding mentors and role models can be a challenge, especially for neurodiverse individuals who may struggle with social interactions or have limited networks. However, there are various strategies that career coaches, educators, and human resources professionals can employ to support their neurodiverse clients in seeking these important relationships. One approach is to leverage existing networks, such as professional organizations or alumni associations, to connect individuals with potential mentors or role models. Another strategy is to encourage individuals to reach out to individuals within their field of interest through social media platforms or professional networking events.

Additionally, it is essential to consider the unique needs and preferences of neurodiverse individuals when connecting them with mentors and role models. Some individuals may benefit from mentors who have a similar neurodiversity, while others may prefer mentors who have successfully navigated similar career paths. It is crucial to facilitate open and honest communication between the mentor and mentee, ensuring that the relationship is mutually beneficial and supportive.

Overall, seeking mentors and role models is a critical component of career coaching and development for neurodiverse individuals. By providing guidance, inspiration, and support, mentors and role models can help neurodiverse individuals overcome challenges, navigate their career paths, and achieve their full potential. By employing effective strategies for finding and cultivating these relationships, career coaches, educators, human resources professionals, and others involved in supporting the career development of neurodiverse individuals can play a vital role in empowering and enabling their clients for success.

Continuing Education and Skill Development

In the ever-evolving world of work, continuous learning and skill development have become essential for career success. This is especially true for neurodiverse individuals, who may face unique challenges and require tailored approaches to their professional development. In this subchapter, we will explore the importance of continuing education and skill development for neurodiverse individuals and provide practical strategies for career coaches, educators, human resources professionals, and others involved in supporting their career journeys.

Neurodiverse individuals possess a range of talents, abilities, and perspectives that can greatly benefit the workplace. However, they may also encounter specific barriers that can hinder their career growth. By focusing on continuing education and skill development, we can help bridge these gaps and empower neurodiverse individuals to reach their full potential.

One key aspect of continuing education is identifying the individual's specific learning style and preferences. Neurodiverse individuals often have unique ways of processing information and acquiring knowledge. By understanding their preferred learning methods, coaches and educators can tailor their teaching strategies to match their needs. This may involve providing visual aids, hands-on activities, or breaking down complex concepts into smaller, more manageable parts.

Additionally, it is important to create a supportive and inclusive learning environment. Neurodiverse individuals may benefit from clear instructions, structured schedules, and ample opportunities for practice and repetition. Providing them with constructive feedback and recognizing their achievements can also boost their confidence and motivation to continue learning.

Skill development is another crucial aspect to address in the journey of neurodiverse individuals' career success. Identifying and enhancing their strengths can help them excel in their chosen fields. Coaches and professionals can conduct assessments to uncover their unique skills and talents, and then work with them to further develop these areas of expertise. This could involve offering specialized training programs, workshops, or mentorship opportunities.

Furthermore, it is important to encourage neurodiverse individuals to embrace a growth mindset. By instilling the belief that abilities can be developed through dedication and hard work, coaches and educators can help them overcome challenges and setbacks. This mindset shift can empower them to take ownership of their learning and skill development, fostering a sense of empowerment and independence.

In conclusion, continuing education and skill development are vital components of career coaching and development for neurodiverse individuals. By understanding their unique learning styles, creating inclusive learning environments, and focusing on their strengths, we can empower them to thrive in their chosen careers. Together, we can build a more inclusive and diverse workforce that celebrates and embraces the differences of all individuals.

Overcoming Career Challenges and Obstacles

In the journey towards career success, individuals with neurodiverse conditions often encounter unique challenges that can impede their progress. However, with the right guidance and support, these individuals can overcome these hurdles and flourish in their chosen fields. This subchapter, "Overcoming Career Challenges and Obstacles," aims to provide valuable insights and strategies to career coaches, educators, human resources professionals, and others involved in supporting the career development of neurodiverse individuals.

One of the initial steps in aiding neurodiverse individuals to overcome career challenges is understanding their specific strengths and challenges. Each neurodiverse condition brings a distinct set of skills and abilities that can be harnessed for success. By identifying these strengths and nurturing them, career coaches can assist individuals in establishing a robust foundation for their careers.

However, it's also crucial to address the obstacles neurodiverse individuals may face in the workplace. These hurdles may involve difficulties with communication, social interactions, executive functioning skills, and sensory sensitivities. Offering targeted interventions and accommodations, such as assistive technologies, workplace mentors, and clear communication strategies, empowers career coaches to help individuals navigate these challenges and foster an inclusive work environment.

Another essential aspect of overcoming career challenges involves fostering self-advocacy skills. Neurodiverse individuals may encounter difficulties expressing their needs or seeking accommodations. Empowering them to advocate for themselves enables career coaches to aid individuals in asserting their rights and creating a supportive network within their workplace.

Moreover, addressing the emotional and psychological aspects of career development for neurodiverse individuals is vital. Many individuals may grapple with anxiety, depression, or low self-esteem while navigating their careers. Providing emotional support, encouraging self-care practices, and promoting a growth mindset helps career coaches assist individuals in building resilience and overcoming these emotional barriers.

This subchapter also explores the significance of inclusive workplace practices and the role of employers and colleagues in supporting the career development of neurodiverse individuals. By fostering a culture of diversity and inclusion, organizations can create a supportive environment where individuals can thrive and realize their full potential.

In conclusion, "Overcoming Career Challenges and Obstacles" offers valuable insights and strategies for career coaches, educators, human resources professionals, and others involved in supporting the career development of neurodiverse individuals. Understanding strengths, addressing challenges, fostering self-advocacy skills, and promoting inclusive workplace practices empower neurodiverse individuals to surmount obstacles and achieve career success.

CHAPTER 7

Supporting Neurodiverse Individuals in the Workplace

―――――――――――

Providing Ongoing Coaching and Support

In the journey towards career success for neurodiverse individuals, ongoing coaching and support play a crucial role. Recognizing and embracing differences is just the first step; it is equally important to provide continuous guidance and assistance to help these individuals navigate their career paths effectively. This subchapter aims to delve into the significance of providing ongoing coaching and support for neurodiverse individuals and the strategies that career coaches, educators, human resources professionals, and other stakeholders can employ to empower and foster independence in their journey.

One key aspect of ongoing coaching and support is establishing a strong mentorship program. Mentors offer valuable guidance, support, and encouragement to neurodiverse individuals, helping them identify their strengths, overcome challenges, and set achievable career goals. These mentors, often experienced professionals who have successfully navigated their own careers while embracing their neurodiversity, can share experiences and provide advice, enabling neurodiverse individuals to build the confidence and skills necessary for success in their chosen career paths.

Additionally, ongoing coaching and support should extend beyond the traditional workplace environment. Neurodiverse individuals often face unique challenges related to communication, social interactions, and sensory sensitivities. Career coaches and educators should collaborate with employers to create inclusive work environments that accommodate these needs. This may involve providing additional training and resources for colleagues and supervisors, ensuring that neurodiverse individuals receive the necessary support to succeed.

Furthermore, ongoing coaching and support should focus on promoting self-advocacy and independence. Neurodiverse individuals should be encouraged to communicate their needs, preferences, and career aspirations openly. Career coaches can work with them to develop effective communication skills, assertiveness, and self-confidence. It is essential to empower neurodiverse individuals to take ownership of their career development and make informed decisions about their professional lives.

Finally, ongoing coaching and support should embrace a holistic approach. Neurodiverse individuals often possess unique talents and perspectives that can bring immense value to organizations. Therefore, career coaches and educators should help them identify and leverage these strengths, enabling them to find fulfilling and meaningful career paths that align with their interests and abilities.

In conclusion, providing ongoing coaching and support is vital for the career success of neurodiverse individuals. By establishing mentorship programs, creating inclusive work environments, promoting self-advocacy and independence, and embracing a holistic approach, career coaches, educators, human resources professionals, and others involved in supporting the career development of neurodiverse individuals can empower them to overcome challenges and achieve their full potential.

Promoting Work-Life Balance

Work-life balance is a crucial aspect of overall well-being and is especially important for neurodiverse individuals. In this subchapter, we will explore the significance of work-life balance and provide practical strategies for promoting it among neurodiverse individuals.

Neurodiverse individuals often face unique challenges when it comes to managing their personal and professional lives. They may experience difficulties in navigating social interactions, sensory sensitivities, and managing their time effectively. These challenges can make it even more essential to prioritize work-life balance in order to maintain good mental health and performance.

One key strategy for promoting work-life balance is helping neurodiverse individuals establish clear boundaries between work and personal life. This can be achieved by encouraging them to set specific working hours and stick to them, avoiding work-related tasks during personal time, and creating a designated workspace to separate work from home life. By establishing these boundaries, they can better manage their time and reduce stress.

Another important aspect of work-life balance is self-care. Neurodiverse individuals may have unique self-care needs, such as sensory self-regulation techniques or engaging in special interests and hobbies. Career coaches can guide them in identifying self-care activities that work best for their specific needs and incorporate them into their daily routines. This can help reduce burnout, boost productivity, and enhance overall well-being.

Flexibility is also crucial for promoting work-life balance among neurodiverse individuals. Employers and educators can play a vital role in accommodating their needs by offering flexible working hours, adjustable workspaces, and remote work options. Providing these accommodations not only supports work-life balance but also enables neurodiverse individuals to thrive in their careers.

Additionally, career coaches can help neurodiverse individuals develop effective time-management skills. This can involve teaching them how to prioritize tasks, break them down into smaller, manageable steps, and utilize organizational tools and techniques. By improving their time-management skills, they can better balance their workload, reduce overwhelm, and create more time for personal life activities.

In conclusion, promoting work-life balance is crucial for the overall well-being and success of neurodiverse individuals. By helping them establish boundaries, prioritize self-care, and develop effective time-management skills, career coaches and other professionals can support their journey towards a balanced and fulfilling life. Embracing work-life balance not only enhances their mental health but also enables them to excel in their careers and personal pursuits.

Addressing Workplace Bullying and Discrimination

Workplace bullying and discrimination are unfortunate realities that many individuals, especially those who are neurodiverse, face in their professional lives. This subchapter aims to shed light on the issue and provide strategies for career coaches, educators, human resources professionals, and others involved in supporting the career development of neurodiverse individuals to address and combat these challenges effectively.

Bullying and discrimination can have severe negative impacts on the well-being, confidence, and career progression of neurodiverse individuals. It is crucial for all professionals who support these individuals to understand the signs of bullying and discrimination and be equipped with tools to intervene and create inclusive work environments.

The first step in addressing workplace bullying and discrimination is to educate both employers and employees about neurodiversity and the unique strengths and challenges of neurodiverse individuals. By raising awareness and promoting acceptance, we can create a more inclusive and understanding workplace culture.

Next, it is essential to establish clear policies and procedures for reporting and addressing incidents of bullying and discrimination. These policies should outline the consequences for such behavior and provide a safe and confidential reporting mechanism. Emphasizing a zero-tolerance approach sends a strong message that bullying and discrimination will not be tolerated.

Career coaches, educators, and human resources professionals should also focus on developing the self-advocacy skills of neurodiverse individuals. Encouraging open communication and teaching assertiveness techniques can empower them to speak up against bullying and discrimination, while also equipping them with the skills to address conflicts in a constructive manner.

Additionally, providing training and resources to managers and colleagues on neurodiversity and inclusive practices can foster a more supportive work environment. By promoting empathy, understanding, and accommodation, we can create a workplace culture that values and embraces differences.

Finally, career coaches and other professionals supporting neurodiverse individuals should collaborate with employers to ensure reasonable accommodations are implemented. These accommodations may include flexible work arrangements, modified job tasks, or additional support to ensure equal opportunities for career development and success.

In conclusion, addressing workplace bullying and discrimination is crucial for the career success and well-being of neurodiverse individuals. By raising awareness, establishing clear policies, fostering self-advocacy, providing training, and promoting reasonable accommodations, career coaches, educators, human resources professionals, and others involved in supporting neurodiverse individuals can create inclusive work environments where everyone can thrive.

Fostering a Positive and Inclusive Organizational Culture

Creating a positive and inclusive organizational culture is crucial for the career success of neurodiverse individuals. In this subchapter, we will explore the various strategies and approaches that career coaches, educators, human resources professionals, and others involved in supporting the career development of neurodiverse individuals can implement to foster such a culture.

First and foremost, it is important to understand and appreciate the unique strengths and abilities that neurodiverse individuals bring to the workplace. By recognizing and valuing their diverse perspectives, innovative thinking, and attention to detail, organizations can create an environment that celebrates differences rather than viewing them as obstacles.

To foster a positive and inclusive culture, organizations should prioritize the implementation of inclusive policies and practices. This involves developing and enforcing equal opportunity and anti-discrimination policies, ensuring that all employees are treated fairly and respectfully. Additionally, providing reasonable accommodations and support services tailored to the specific needs of neurodiverse individuals can help level the playing field and enable them to thrive in their chosen careers.

Education and awareness are also vital components of fostering a positive and inclusive culture. By conducting training sessions and workshops, organizations can help employees understand the different neurodiverse conditions and learn how to interact and communicate effectively with their neurodiverse colleagues. This not only promotes empathy and understanding but also contributes to the overall inclusivity of the workplace.

Furthermore, creating support networks and mentorship programs within the organization can be highly beneficial. Pairing neurodiverse individuals with mentors who have experience in navigating the workplace can provide valuable guidance, support, and opportunities for growth. These networks also facilitate the sharing of experiences and best practices, fostering a sense of belonging and community.

Finally, organizations should regularly assess and evaluate their progress in creating a positive and inclusive culture. This can be done through anonymous surveys, focus groups, or feedback mechanisms, allowing employees to voice their opinions and concerns. By actively seeking input from neurodiverse individuals, organizations can identify areas for improvement and implement necessary changes to further enhance inclusivity.

In conclusion, fostering a positive and inclusive organizational culture is essential for the career success of neurodiverse individuals. By appreciating their unique strengths, implementing inclusive policies, providing education and support, and creating mentorship programs, organizations can create an environment that celebrates diversity and enables neurodiverse individuals to reach their full potential.

Celebrating Successes and Recognizing Contributions

In the journey towards empowering and supporting the career development of neurodiverse individuals, it is crucial to highlight the importance of celebrating successes and recognizing contributions. This subchapter delves into the significance of acknowledging achievements and the positive impact it has on the lives of neurodiverse individuals.

Neurodiverse individuals, with their unique set of strengths and abilities, often face various challenges in the workplace. However, it is essential to shift the focus from these challenges to the accomplishments and contributions they bring to their respective fields. By highlighting their successes, we can create a more inclusive and supportive work environment that values diversity.

Celebrating successes not only boosts the confidence and self-esteem of neurodiverse individuals but also helps in fostering a sense of belonging and acceptance. When their achievements are recognized, it sends a powerful message that their efforts are valued and appreciated. This recognition can lead to increased motivation and a willingness to take on new challenges, ultimately driving career growth and advancement.

Furthermore, celebrating successes can have a ripple effect on the entire organization. It creates a culture of appreciation and positivity, encouraging other employees to recognize and celebrate each other's achievements. This, in turn, promotes a collaborative and supportive work environment where everyone feels valued and included.

Recognizing contributions goes hand in hand with celebrating successes. It involves acknowledging the unique skills, talents, and perspectives that neurodiverse individuals bring to the table. By recognizing their contributions, we create opportunities for them to showcase their abilities and make meaningful contributions to the organization's success.

In this subchapter, we explore various strategies for celebrating successes and recognizing contributions. From implementing recognition programs and awards to creating platforms for sharing success stories, we provide practical guidance for career coaches, educators, human resources professionals, and others involved in supporting the career development of neurodiverse individuals.

By embracing the practice of celebrating successes and recognizing contributions, we can create a more inclusive and empowering environment for neurodiverse individuals. Together, let us champion their achievements and create a future where diversity is not only accepted but celebrated in the workplace.

CHAPTER 8

Collaborating with Educators and Human Resources Professionals

Training Educators on Neurodiversity

In recent years, there has been a growing recognition of the importance of neurodiversity in education. Neurodiversity refers to the idea that neurological differences, such as autism, ADHD, dyslexia, and other conditions, are simply natural variations of the human brain. Instead of viewing these differences as deficits, neurodiversity celebrates the unique strengths and perspectives that neurodiverse individuals bring to the table.

For educators, understanding and embracing neurodiversity is crucial to creating inclusive and supportive learning environments. By recognizing the diverse needs and abilities of neurodiverse students, educators can provide the necessary accommodations and support to help them thrive academically and socially.

To effectively support neurodiverse students, educators must undergo training that focuses on understanding the various neurological differences, their impact on learning, and strategies for creating inclusive classrooms. This subchapter aims to provide valuable insights and practical guidance on training educators to embrace neurodiversity.

The first step in training educators on neurodiversity is raising awareness. Many educators may have limited knowledge or misconceptions about neurodiverse conditions. By providing accurate information about different neurodiverse conditions, their strengths, challenges, and the impact they have on learning, educators can develop a better understanding and empathy towards neurodiverse students.

Next, educators should be introduced to various teaching strategies and accommodations that can be implemented in the classroom. Differentiated instruction, visual aids, sensory-friendly environments, and assistive technologies are just a few examples of the strategies that can be used to support neurodiverse learners. Educators need to be equipped with practical tools and techniques that can be tailored to meet the individual needs of neurodiverse students.

Furthermore, it is essential to address the social and emotional aspects of neurodiversity. Educators should be trained on fostering a supportive and inclusive classroom culture that celebrates diversity and promotes empathy and understanding among students. By addressing issues such as bullying, stigma, and social isolation, educators can create safe spaces where neurodiverse students can feel accepted and valued.

Lastly, collaboration and partnership between educators, parents, and other professionals are key to supporting neurodiverse students effectively. Educators should be trained on the importance of establishing open lines of communication with parents, sharing information, and working together to develop individualized education plans that cater to the unique needs of each student.

By training educators on neurodiversity, we can create a more inclusive and supportive educational system that allows neurodiverse individuals to thrive academically and pave their way towards successful careers. Empowering educators with the knowledge and skills to embrace neurodiversity is a crucial step towards creating a more inclusive society that celebrates and values the strengths and contributions of all individuals, regardless of their neurological differences.

Creating Individualized Education Plans (IEPs)

In the journey towards achieving career success, neurodiverse individuals often require additional support and accommodations to help them thrive in educational settings. One effective tool for providing this support is the Individualized Education Plan (IEP). This subchapter explores the importance of creating IEPs and provides practical guidance for career coaches, educators, human resources professionals, and others involved in supporting the career development of neurodiverse individuals.

An IEP is a personalized roadmap that outlines specific goals, accommodations, and services tailored to meet the unique needs of each neurodiverse individual. It is a collaborative process involving various stakeholders, including the individual, their family, educators, and professionals. The primary objective of an IEP is to ensure that neurodiverse individuals receive the necessary support to excel academically and develop the skills required for future career success.

To create an effective IEP, it is crucial to gather comprehensive information about the individual's strengths, challenges, and aspirations. This can be achieved through assessments, interviews, and discussions with the individual, their family, and relevant professionals. By understanding their specific needs, career coaches and educators can identify appropriate accommodations and interventions to support their educational and career goals.

The IEP should include measurable goals that are specific, realistic, and achievable within a given timeframe. These goals should be aligned with the individual's interests and strengths, while also addressing areas of challenge. For example, if a neurodiverse individual has exceptional visual-spatial abilities but struggles with social interactions, the IEP may prioritize developing social skills while leveraging their visual strengths in career exploration activities.

Accommodations and support services should be clearly outlined in the IEP to ensure that neurodiverse individuals can access the resources they need to succeed. These may include extended time for exams, assistive technology, preferential seating, or additional support from special education professionals. The IEP should also establish a system for monitoring progress and periodically reviewing and updating the plan based on the individual's evolving needs.

By creating individualized education plans, career coaches, educators, and other professionals can empower neurodiverse individuals to overcome barriers and reach their full potential. These plans foster a supportive and inclusive educational environment that recognizes and celebrates neurodiversity. Moreover, they lay a strong foundation for successful career development by equipping individuals with the skills, accommodations, and resources they need to thrive in their chosen professions.

In conclusion, the creation of individualized education plans (IEPs) is an essential tool for supporting the career development of neurodiverse individuals. By considering their unique strengths, challenges, and aspirations, career coaches and educators can develop IEPs that provide the necessary accommodations, goals, and support services to help neurodiverse individuals excel academically and prepare for successful careers. Through collaboration and ongoing assessment, these plans can be continuously updated and revised to ensure that they remain effective in meeting the evolving needs of neurodiverse individuals.

Transitioning from School to Work

The transition from school to work can be a challenging process for neurodiverse individuals. As they navigate the complexities of the working world, they may encounter a range of barriers and obstacles that can hinder their career success. However, with the right support and guidance, individuals with neurodiverse conditions can overcome these challenges and thrive in their chosen careers.

This subchapter explores the key considerations and strategies for supporting neurodiverse individuals as they transition from school to work. It provides practical advice and insights for career coaches, educators, human resources professionals, and others involved in the career development of neurodiverse individuals.

Firstly, it is crucial to recognize and understand the unique strengths and challenges that neurodiverse individuals bring to the workplace. Each individual has their own set of skills and abilities that can be harnessed to contribute positively to the workplace. By focusing on their strengths and providing accommodations where necessary, career coaches and educators can help neurodiverse individuals find their niche and excel in their chosen fields.

Secondly, effective communication and collaboration between all stakeholders involved in the transition process is vital. This includes regular dialogue between the individual, their support network, and potential employers. By fostering an open and inclusive dialogue, career coaches and human resources professionals can ensure that the needs of neurodiverse individuals are understood and met in the workplace.

Additionally, providing practical training and support during the transition period can greatly enhance the chances of success. This can include job readiness programs, internships, and mentorship opportunities. By gaining real-world experience and receiving guidance from experienced professionals, neurodiverse individuals can build their confidence and develop the necessary skills to thrive in their chosen careers.

Lastly, fostering an inclusive and supportive work environment is crucial for the long-term success of neurodiverse individuals. This can be achieved through workplace accommodations, such as flexible work arrangements or sensory-friendly spaces. Additionally, promoting awareness and understanding of neurodiversity among colleagues and supervisors can help create a more inclusive and accepting workplace culture.

In conclusion, the transition from school to work is a critical phase for neurodiverse individuals, and it requires the support and guidance of career coaches, educators, human resources professionals, and others involved in their career development. By recognizing their unique strengths, fostering effective communication, providing practical training, and creating inclusive work environments, we can empower neurodiverse individuals to achieve career success and embrace their differences in the workplace.

Collaborating with Human Resources Professionals

In the ever-evolving workplace landscape, collaboration between career coaches, educators, and human resources professionals has become crucial in supporting the career development of neurodiverse individuals. Neurodiverse individuals bring unique perspectives and strengths to the table, and it is imperative for HR professionals to create an inclusive and supportive environment that allows them to thrive.

Human resources professionals play a vital role in the success of neurodiverse individuals by ensuring that policies and practices are inclusive and accommodating. By collaborating with HR professionals, career coaches can gain valuable insights into the company's culture, policies, and procedures, allowing them to tailor their coaching strategies effectively.

One essential aspect of collaboration with HR professionals is the identification and implementation of reasonable accommodations. These accommodations can be instrumental in providing neurodiverse individuals with the necessary support to excel in their careers. HR professionals can provide invaluable guidance on the legal and ethical aspects of accommodations, ensuring that both the individual and the organization benefit from a diverse and inclusive work environment.

Furthermore, HR professionals can assist career coaches in identifying potential job opportunities for neurodiverse individuals. By understanding the specific skills, strengths, and challenges of neurodiverse individuals, HR professionals can help identify roles that align with their abilities and provide the necessary support for success. Additionally, HR professionals can facilitate the creation of inclusive job descriptions and interview processes that take into account the diverse needs of neurodiverse candidates.

Collaboration with HR professionals also extends to the training and development of existing employees. HR professionals can work closely with career coaches to design and implement training programs that promote awareness, understanding, and acceptance of neurodiversity in the workplace. By fostering a culture of inclusivity, HR professionals can create an environment where neurodiverse individuals can reach their full potential and contribute meaningfully to the organization.

In conclusion, collaboration between career coaches and HR professionals is essential for the successful career development of neurodiverse individuals. By working together, these professionals can identify reasonable accommodations, create inclusive job opportunities, and foster a supportive workplace culture. The result is a win-win situation where neurodiverse individuals can thrive professionally, and organizations can benefit from the unique talents and perspectives they bring.

Establishing Partnerships for Long-Term Support

In the journey towards empowering and promoting the independence of neurodiverse individuals, establishing long-term partnerships is crucial. These partnerships play a pivotal role in providing the necessary support and guidance to help neurodiverse individuals thrive in their careers. By bridging the gap between career coaches, educators, human resources professionals, and other stakeholders involved in supporting neurodiverse individuals, these partnerships create a network of resources that can pave the way for long-term success.

One key aspect of establishing partnerships for long-term support is collaboration. Career coaches, educators, and human resources professionals must work together to ensure a holistic approach to supporting neurodiverse individuals. By sharing expertise, resources, and best practices, these individuals can collectively develop strategies that address the specific needs and challenges faced by neurodiverse individuals in their career development.

Building trust and rapport is another important element of these partnerships. Neurodiverse individuals may have unique communication styles or social challenges that require additional understanding and patience. By fostering strong relationships based on trust and empathy, career coaches and other professionals can create a safe and supportive environment for neurodiverse individuals to explore their career aspirations and goals.

Partnerships for long-term support should also extend beyond the immediate career coaching process. It is essential to establish connections with community organizations, employers, and other support networks that can provide ongoing assistance and resources.

These partnerships can help neurodiverse individuals access employment opportunities, internships, mentoring programs, and other avenues for skill development and growth.

Additionally, establishing partnerships should involve continuous learning and professional development. Career coaches, educators, and human resources professionals should stay updated on the latest research, best practices, and innovative approaches in supporting neurodiverse individuals. By attending workshops, conferences, and networking events, professionals can expand their knowledge and expertise, enabling them to better serve the career development needs of neurodiverse individuals.

In conclusion, establishing partnerships for long-term support is crucial in empowering neurodiverse individuals in their career journeys. Collaboration, trust-building, and ongoing learning are key components of these partnerships. By working together, career coaches, educators, human resources professionals, and other stakeholders can create a supportive network that nurtures the unique talents and potential of neurodiverse individuals, ultimately leading to their career success and independence.

CHAPTER 9

Case Studies and Success Stories

John's Journey: From Unemployment to Career Success

In the subchapter titled "John's Journey: From Unemployment to Career Success," we delve into the inspiring story of John, a neurodiverse individual who overcame the challenges of unemployment to achieve a fulfilling and successful career. This chapter aims to provide career coaches, educators, human resources professionals, and others involved in supporting the career development of neurodiverse individuals with valuable insights and strategies to empower and guide their clients towards similar achievements.

John's story is a testament to the power of embracing differences and recognizing the unique strengths and talents that neurodiverse individuals possess. As a career coach, it is crucial to understand the specific needs and challenges faced by neurodiverse individuals in the job market. By acknowledging and addressing these differences, we can create a supportive environment that fosters their career growth.

John's journey began with his struggle to find employment due to the societal biases and misconceptions surrounding neurodiversity. However, with the help of a dedicated career coach, he was able to identify his strengths and skills. Through personalized coaching sessions, John gained a deeper understanding of his unique abilities, such as his exceptional attention to detail, analytical thinking, and creativity.

Armed with this newfound self-awareness, John and his career coach worked together to identify suitable career paths that aligned with his strengths. They explored different industries and job roles that could harness his skills effectively. By leveraging his strengths, John was able to find his niche in a field that valued his abilities and provided a supportive environment.

Throughout John's journey, his career coach played a pivotal role in providing guidance, support, and advocacy. They helped him navigate the job application process, provided interview preparation, and even facilitated workplace accommodations to ensure his success. The career coach also worked closely with employers and HR professionals, educating them on neurodiversity and promoting inclusive hiring practices.

John's story serves as an inspiration for both neurodiverse individuals and those who support their career development. It highlights the importance of individualized coaching and understanding the unique talents and strengths of neurodiverse individuals. By embracing these differences, we can create a more inclusive and diverse workforce that values the contributions of every individual.

In conclusion, "John's Journey: From Unemployment to Career Success" showcases the transformative power of career coaching for neurodiverse individuals. By providing the right support, guidance, and advocacy, career coaches, educators, HR professionals, and others involved in supporting the career development of neurodiverse individuals can empower them to achieve their full potential and find meaningful and fulfilling careers.

Sarah's Story: Overcoming Challenges and Embracing Strengths

Sarah's journey is a testament to the power of resilience, determination, and self-discovery. As a neurodiverse individual, she has faced numerous challenges throughout her life, but through the support of career coaches, educators, and HR professionals, she has been able to overcome these obstacles and embrace her unique strengths.

From a young age, Sarah struggled to fit into traditional educational settings. Her learning style was different from her peers, and she often felt misunderstood and left behind. However, with the guidance of dedicated educators who recognized her potential, Sarah began to discover her strengths and talents. Through personalized teaching methods and accommodations, she was able to thrive academically and gain confidence in her abilities.

As Sarah entered the workforce, new challenges arose. The job application and interview process felt overwhelming, and she often struggled to effectively communicate her skills and experiences. However, with the support of career coaches who specialized in working with neurodiverse individuals, Sarah learned strategies to navigate these hurdles. She discovered the power of self-advocacy, honed her interview skills, and built a network of professionals who saw her potential.

One of the most significant turning points in Sarah's journey was when she embraced her neurodiversity as a strength rather than a limitation. Through self-reflection and self-acceptance, she recognized that her unique perspective and problem-solving skills were assets in the workplace. With this newfound confidence, she pursued opportunities that aligned with her strengths and passions.

Sarah's story serves as an inspiration to others in the neurodiverse community. It highlights the importance of providing tailored support and accommodations to help individuals overcome challenges and reach their full potential. By understanding and embracing neurodiversity, career coaches, educators, and HR professionals can create inclusive environments that foster the success of all individuals.

In conclusion, Sarah's journey showcases the transformative power of career coaching and development for neurodiverse individuals. By addressing their unique challenges and harnessing their strengths, these individuals can overcome obstacles and achieve their career goals. Through the collective efforts of career coaches, educators, and HR professionals, we can empower and support the neurodiverse community in their pursuit of success and fulfillment in the workplace.

Alex's Path: Navigating a Neurodiverse-Friendly Workplace

In this subchapter, we will delve into the essential strategies and tools for creating a neurodiverse-friendly workplace environment, specifically tailored to support individuals like Alex. Alex, a neurodiverse individual, possesses unique strengths and abilities that can greatly contribute to the success of any organization. However, they may face certain challenges in navigating the traditional workplace structure.

To begin with, it is crucial for employers and colleagues to understand and appreciate the concept of neurodiversity. Neurodiversity recognizes and values the wide range of neurological differences that exist in society, including autism, ADHD, dyslexia, and other conditions. By embracing neurodiversity, organizations can tap into the diverse talents and perspectives of their workforce, fostering a more inclusive and innovative work environment.

Creating a neurodiverse-friendly workplace starts with providing appropriate accommodations and support. This can include flexible work hours, sensory-friendly workspaces, and clear communication channels. Employers should engage in open dialogue with neurodiverse individuals like Alex, understanding their unique needs and preferences. By making reasonable adjustments to the work environment, employers can empower individuals to thrive and contribute effectively.

Another crucial element is promoting awareness and understanding among colleagues. Educating the workforce about neurodiversity can help dispel myths and misconceptions, reducing stigma and fostering an inclusive culture. Training programs and workshops can be conducted to enhance empathy, communication, and collaboration skills. By creating a safe and supportive environment, employers can encourage neurodiverse individuals to be their authentic selves and fully participate in the workplace.

Furthermore, career coaches and educators play a critical role in supporting neurodiverse individuals like Alex. By utilizing person-centered coaching techniques, coaches can help individuals identify their strengths, interests, and career goals. Coaches can also assist in developing self-advocacy and self-disclosure skills, helping individuals navigate the disclosure process in the workplace, if they choose to do so.

In conclusion, creating a neurodiverse-friendly workplace requires a collective effort from employers, colleagues, and career coaches. By embracing neurodiversity, providing appropriate accommodations, promoting awareness, and offering individualized support, organizations can unlock the full potential of neurodiverse individuals like Alex. A neurodiverse-friendly workplace not only benefits individuals but also leads to enhanced innovation, productivity, and overall success for the organization.

Emily's Experience: Thriving in a Supportive Environment

In this subchapter, we delve into the inspiring journey of Emily, a neurodiverse individual, who has successfully navigated her career path with the help of a supportive environment. Emily's experience sheds light on the importance of creating a nurturing and inclusive workplace that fosters the growth and development of neurodiverse individuals.

Emily's story begins with her struggle to find employment that aligned with her unique strengths and abilities. Like many neurodiverse individuals, she faced various barriers and prejudices while searching for suitable job opportunities. However, her life took a positive turn when she connected with a career coach who understood her needs and aspirations.

With the guidance of her career coach, Emily was able to identify her strengths and interests, and explore career options that complemented her skillset. Together, they conducted thorough assessments and identified potential industries that valued neurodiversity and offered supportive work environments.

Once Emily secured a position in a company that embraced diversity and provided necessary accommodations, she began to thrive. The supportive environment allowed her to showcase her exceptional attention to detail, pattern recognition skills, and ability to think outside the box. Her contributions were not only recognized but also celebrated by her colleagues and superiors.

The supportive environment not only enabled Emily to excel in her role but also empowered her to grow both personally and professionally. She was given opportunities for continuous learning and professional development, which further enhanced her skills and confidence. Through mentorship programs, she had access to experienced professionals who provided guidance and encouragement along her career path.

Emily's success story highlights the transformative impact of a supportive workplace environment for neurodiverse individuals. It emphasizes the need for employers and career coaches to create inclusive spaces that embrace diversity and provide the necessary resources and accommodations. By doing so, they can unlock the tremendous potential and unique talents of neurodiverse individuals, ultimately benefiting both the individual and the organization.

As career coaches, educators, and HR professionals, it is crucial that we understand the significance of nurturing a supportive environment for neurodiverse individuals. By doing so, we can help them overcome challenges, thrive in their careers, and contribute meaningfully to their respective fields. Emily's experience serves as a testament to the transformative power of supportive workplaces and the positive outcomes that can be achieved when individuals are given the opportunity to excel in an inclusive environment.

In conclusion, "Emily's Experience: Thriving in a Supportive Environment" showcases the journey of a neurodiverse individual who found success and fulfillment in a workplace that embraced diversity and provided the necessary accommodations. This subchapter emphasizes the importance of creating inclusive work environments and highlights the transformative impact it can have on the career development of neurodiverse individuals.

Mike's Triumph: From Self-Doubt to Confidence

In the subchapter titled "Mike's Triumph: From Self-Doubt to Confidence" from the book "Embracing Differences: Career Coaching for Neurodiverse Individuals," we delve into the inspiring journey of Mike, a neurodiverse individual who overcame self-doubt and transformed into a confident professional.

Mike's story begins with his struggle to find his place in the professional world. As a neurodiverse individual, he faced unique challenges in understanding social cues, managing stress, and adapting to new environments. These obstacles led to a lack of confidence and self-doubt that hindered his career development.

However, with the help of a knowledgeable and empathetic career coach, Mike embarked on a transformative journey towards empowerment and independence. The coach recognized Mike's unique strengths and abilities, focusing on his exceptional attention to detail, strong analytical skills, and unwavering dedication. By shifting the perspective from deficits to strengths, Mike began to see himself in a new light.

The coach worked closely with Mike to develop strategies that played to his strengths while addressing his challenges. Through personalized career coaching sessions, Mike learned effective communication techniques, stress management strategies, and problem-solving skills. The coach also guided Mike in developing self-advocacy abilities, teaching him how to effectively communicate his needs and accommodations to employers.

As Mike gained confidence in his abilities, the coach encouraged him to explore various career paths that aligned with his interests and strengths. Together, they identified industries and roles where his unique skill set could thrive. The coach also helped Mike build a powerful network, connecting him with professionals who appreciated the value of neurodiversity in the workplace.

Through perseverance and the unwavering support of his coach, Mike began to land interviews and job offers. With each successful step, his self-doubt slowly transformed into confidence. Mike's journey serves as a testament to the power of personalized career coaching for neurodiverse individuals.

The subchapter "Mike's Triumph: From Self-Doubt to Confidence" in "Embracing Differences: Career Coaching for Neurodiverse Individuals" highlights the importance of recognizing and embracing the unique strengths and abilities of neurodiverse individuals. It showcases how career coaches, educators, human resources professionals, and others involved in supporting the career development of neurodiverse individuals can empower them to overcome self-doubt and achieve career success. By providing personalized guidance, strategies, and support, professionals in these roles can help neurodiverse individuals like Mike unlock their full potential and thrive in the workplace.

CHAPTER 10

Empowering Neurodiverse Individuals for Long-Term Success

Encouraging Self-Advocacy and Independence

Neurodiverse individuals possess unique talents and perspectives that can greatly contribute to the workplace. However, they often face challenges in navigating the professional world due to their diverse cognitive profiles. As career coaches, educators, human resources professionals, and other individuals involved in supporting the career development of neurodiverse individuals, it is crucial for us to empower and guide them towards self-advocacy and independence.

Self-advocacy is the ability to speak up and advocate for one's needs, rights, and interests. For neurodiverse individuals, developing self-advocacy skills is particularly important as it helps them navigate the often complex and overwhelming job market. One way to encourage self-advocacy is by fostering a supportive and inclusive environment that values neurodiversity. This can be achieved by providing educational resources, workshops, and training sessions that promote awareness and understanding of neurodiversity among colleagues and employers.

In addition, it is essential to work with neurodiverse individuals individually to help them identify their strengths, weaknesses, and specific needs. By understanding their unique cognitive profiles, we can assist them in developing strategies to effectively communicate their strengths and accommodation requirements to potential employers. This might include creating personalized resumes, cover letters, and interview preparation techniques that highlight their abilities while addressing their challenges.

Empowering neurodiverse individuals to become self-advocates also involves teaching them self-awareness and self-acceptance. By helping them embrace their neurodivergent traits as strengths, they can build confidence and resilience in the face of potential barriers. Through coaching, we can guide them in recognizing their strengths, setting realistic goals, and developing a positive mindset that enables them to overcome challenges and seize opportunities.

Promoting independence is another essential aspect of supporting the career development of neurodiverse individuals. Independence means equipping them with the skills and resources necessary to navigate the professional world autonomously. This can involve providing guidance on networking, job searching, and career planning. By teaching them how to conduct informational interviews, build professional connections, and effectively search for job opportunities, we enable them to take control of their career paths.

Finally, ongoing support and mentorship are crucial for neurodiverse individuals to maintain their independence and self-advocacy skills. As career coaches, educators, and human resources professionals, we can continue to be a source of guidance and encouragement throughout their professional journey. By offering regular check-ins, providing resources, and connecting them with mentors who have experienced similar challenges, we can ensure that they have the support they need to thrive in their careers.

In conclusion, encouraging self-advocacy and independence among neurodiverse individuals is essential for their career success. By fostering a supportive environment, assisting them in understanding their unique strengths and needs, promoting self-awareness and acceptance, and equipping them with the necessary skills, we can empower them to navigate the professional world confidently and independently. Through our guidance and ongoing support, we can help neurodiverse individuals embrace their differences and make meaningful contributions to the workforce.

Building Resilience and Coping Skills

In the journey towards career success, building resilience and developing effective coping skills is crucial for neurodiverse individuals. Navigating the professional world can be challenging for those with neurodiverse conditions such as autism, ADHD, dyslexia, and others. However, with the right strategies and support, individuals can overcome obstacles and thrive in their chosen careers.

Resilience is the ability to bounce back from setbacks and adapt to change. It is an essential skill for anyone, but particularly important for neurodiverse individuals who may face unique challenges in the workplace. Building resilience involves developing a positive mindset, embracing failures as opportunities for growth, and cultivating a strong support network.

One effective strategy for building resilience is to focus on strengths and abilities. Neurodiverse individuals often possess unique talents and skills that can be harnessed for career success. By recognizing and capitalizing on these strengths, individuals can boost their confidence and develop a sense of purpose. Career coaches can play a vital role in helping individuals identify their strengths and align them with suitable career paths.

Another crucial aspect of building resilience is developing effective coping skills. Neurodiverse individuals may experience heightened sensitivity to certain stimuli, social challenges, or difficulties with time management and organization. By learning coping strategies tailored to their specific needs, individuals can better manage stress, regulate emotions, and maintain focus in the workplace.

Coping skills can include techniques such as mindfulness meditation, deep breathing exercises, time management tools, and sensory regulation strategies. Career coaches, educators, and human resources professionals can provide guidance on these techniques, helping individuals develop customized coping plans that address their unique challenges.

Support networks are also vital in building resilience and coping skills. By connecting with peers, mentors, and support groups, neurodiverse individuals can find a safe space to share experiences, gain insights, and receive encouragement. In addition to traditional support networks, online communities and social media platforms can provide valuable resources and connections for individuals seeking guidance and support.

By integrating these strategies into their coaching and support practices, career coaches, educators, and human resources professionals can empower neurodiverse individuals to build resilience and develop effective coping skills. With the right tools and support, individuals can embrace their differences, overcome challenges, and achieve career success on their terms.

Continuous Professional Development

In the fast-paced and ever-changing world of work, it is essential for career coaches, educators, human resources professionals, and other individuals involved in supporting the career development of neurodiverse individuals to engage in continuous professional development (CPD). CPD is a lifelong learning process that helps professionals enhance their knowledge, skills, and abilities to stay current and effective in their respective fields.

For professionals primarily focused on career coaching and development for neurodiverse individuals, CPD plays a crucial role in staying abreast of the latest research, best practices, and strategies for supporting their clients. As the understanding of neurodiversity continues to evolve, it is important for these professionals to stay informed about the unique strengths, challenges, and needs of neurodiverse individuals in the workplace.

One aspect of CPD that is particularly relevant for career coaches and professionals working with neurodiverse individuals is the ongoing development of knowledge and skills related to neurodiversity. This includes understanding the different types of neurodivergent conditions such as autism, ADHD, dyslexia, and others, as well as the specific challenges and strengths associated with each condition. By staying up-to-date with the latest research and information, professionals can better tailor their coaching and support to meet the individual needs of their neurodiverse clients.

Additionally, CPD provides an opportunity for professionals to enhance their coaching and communication skills. Effective coaching requires active listening, empathy, and the ability to ask powerful questions. By continually honing these skills, professionals can create a safe and supportive environment for their neurodiverse clients to explore their career goals, identify their strengths, and overcome challenges. CPD can also provide professionals with the opportunity to learn new coaching techniques and tools that can be specifically adapted to support neurodiverse individuals in their career development journey.

Furthermore, CPD can help professionals stay current with the latest trends and innovations in the workplace. This includes understanding the changing nature of work, emerging industries, and the skills required for success in the digital age. By staying informed about these trends, professionals can better guide their neurodiverse clients in developing the skills and competencies necessary for career success.

In conclusion, continuous professional development is essential for career coaches, educators, human resources professionals, and others involved in supporting the career development of neurodiverse individuals. By engaging in CPD, professionals can enhance their knowledge, skills, and abilities to better understand and support the unique needs of their neurodiverse clients. Through ongoing learning and development, professionals can ensure they are providing the most effective and up-to-date coaching and support, ultimately empowering neurodiverse individuals to achieve their career goals and thrive in the workplace.

Establishing Work-Life Balance for Neurodiverse Individuals

Finding a healthy work-life balance is crucial for everyone, including neurodiverse individuals who might encounter unique challenges in both the workplace and their personal lives. This subchapter will explore strategies and techniques tailored specifically to help neurodiverse individuals establish a better work-life balance.

Understanding Personal Needs: The first step in achieving work-life balance involves recognizing and understanding one's own needs and limitations. Neurodiverse individuals may have distinct preferences regarding work hours, the work environment, and personal time. Career coaches can assist in identifying these specific needs to create a more balanced lifestyle.

Setting Boundaries: Clear boundaries between work and personal life are crucial. Career coaches can help neurodiverse individuals set realistic goals and expectations, enabling them to manage their time and energy effectively. Techniques such as time blocking, allocating specific time slots for work-related tasks, personal activities, and relaxation, can be beneficial.

Advocating for Accommodations: Neurodiverse individuals may require workplace accommodations to support their work-life balance. Career coaches can aid in identifying and requesting these accommodations, such as flexible work hours, remote work options, or noise-cancelling headphones. Advocating for these needs helps create an environment conducive to balance and productivity.

Stress Management: Stress significantly affects work-life balance, especially for neurodiverse individuals sensitive to environmental stimuli. Career coaches can teach stress management techniques like deep breathing exercises, mindfulness practices, and physical activities to help them maintain balance and cope with workplace challenges.

Building Support Networks: Encouraging the development of supportive relationships is crucial for neurodiverse individuals in both work and personal spheres. Career coaches can guide them in developing strong communication skills, nurturing positive relationships with colleagues, and seeking out mentors or support groups. These networks offer emotional support and practical advice, contributing to improved work-life balance.

By implementing these strategies, neurodiverse individuals can establish a healthy work-life balance that supports their overall well-being and career success. The roles of career coaches, educators, and HR professionals are pivotal in supporting neurodiverse individuals in their journey towards achieving balance and fulfillment in all aspects of their lives.

Nurturing a Supportive Community for Neurodiverse Individuals

In the journey towards career success for neurodiverse individuals, cultivating and nurturing a supportive community stands as a paramount factor. This subchapter delves into the importance of building a robust network of support and collaboration, offering strategies for career coaches, educators, human resources professionals, and others involved in aiding the career development of neurodiverse individuals.

A supportive community serves as an invaluable resource for neurodiverse individuals, offering emotional support, guidance, and avenues for personal growth. It is crucial for career coaches and professionals to acknowledge the unique challenges faced by neurodiverse individuals and actively foster a sense of belonging and inclusivity. By establishing a safe and accepting environment, individuals feel empowered to freely express themselves, share experiences, and learn from each other.

One effective strategy for nurturing such a community is through mentorship programs. Mentors, whether neurotypical or neurodiverse themselves, offer guidance, encouragement, and practical advice in navigating the complexities of the workplace. Connecting neurodiverse individuals with mentors who have successfully overcome similar challenges provides valuable insights and builds confidence in their abilities.

Additionally, fostering a supportive community involves promoting collaboration and teamwork. Career coaches and educators can facilitate group activities, team-building exercises, and networking events that encourage interaction and relationship-building among neurodiverse individuals. Working together on projects, exchanging ideas, and collaborating on problem-solving cultivates crucial interpersonal skills and establishes a robust support system.

Moreover, providing platforms for neurodiverse individuals to showcase their talents and skills is essential. Organizing events, workshops, or conferences that highlight their achievements and contributions allows the broader community to recognize and appreciate their unique perspectives and abilities. This not only enhances their self-esteem but also raises awareness and encourages acceptance in society at large.

To nurture a 'supportive community, it is imperative for career coaches, educators, human resources professionals, and others to continually educate themselves about the specific needs and challenges faced by neurodiverse individuals. Staying informed about the latest research, best practices, and available resources enables them to provide tailored support and guidance, facilitating the thriving of neurodiverse individuals in their careers.

In conclusion, nurturing a supportive community stands as a vital element in the career coaching and development of neurodiverse individuals. Through creating inclusive environments, leveraging mentorship programs, promoting collaboration, and providing recognition opportunities, career professionals empower neurodiverse individuals to unleash their full potential and achieve sustained career success.

APPENDIX A

Resources for Neurodiverse Individuals

In this appendix, you will find a comprehensive list of resources specifically curated to support the career development and success of neurodiverse individuals. These resources have been carefully selected to provide a wide range of tools, strategies, and support networks that can empower and guide both career coaches and neurodiverse individuals on their journey towards career success.

1. Websites and Online Communities:

- Neurodiversity Hub: An online platform that offers a wealth of resources, articles, and forums discussing topics related to neurodiversity in the workplace.

- Autism at Work: A website dedicated to promoting and supporting the inclusion of individuals on the autism spectrum in the workforce, offering valuable insights, success stories, and resources.

- Job Accommodation Network (JAN): Provides information on workplace accommodations, disability-related legislation, and resources for individuals with disabilities.

2. Tools and Assessments:

- Strengths-Based Assessments: Resources that help identify and capitalize on the unique strengths and talents of neurodiverse individuals, such as the CliftonStrengths assessment or the VIA Character Strengths survey.

- Career Interest Inventories: Online tools that assist in exploring and matching individual interests with potential career paths, such as the Holland Code or the O*NET Interest Profiler.

3. Training and Education:

- Neurodiversity in the Workplace Training Programs: Organizations that offer training programs on neurodiversity awareness, inclusion, and best practices for employers, such as Neurodiversity Works or Autism @ Work Playbook.

- Online Courses: Platforms that provide specialized courses on topics like job interviewing skills, workplace communication, and self-advocacy for neurodiverse individuals, such as Udemy or Coursera.

4. Support Networks and Organizations:

- Autistic Self-Advocacy Network (ASAN): A nonprofit organization that promotes the rights and inclusion of autistic individuals, offering resources, advocacy, and community support.

- National Alliance on Mental Illness (NAMI): A grassroots mental health organization that provides support, education, and resources for individuals with mental health conditions, including those on the neurodiverse spectrum.

- Disability:IN: A global nonprofit network that empowers organizations to create inclusive workplaces and actively hires and supports individuals with disabilities.

In conclusion, this appendix serves as a valuable reference point for career coaches, educators, human resources professionals, and others involved in supporting the career development of neurodiverse individuals. The provided resources offer a wealth of knowledge, tools, and support networks that can enhance the empowerment and independence of neurodiverse individuals in their pursuit of career success. By utilizing these resources, professionals in the field can effectively coach and guide neurodiverse individuals towards fulfilling and meaningful careers.

APPENDIX B

Websites and Tools for Career Coaches

In today's digital age, career coaches and professionals supporting the career development of neurodiverse individuals have a wealth of resources at their fingertips. This appendix presents a curated list of websites and tools that are primarily focused on career coaching and development for neurodiverse individuals.

1. Neurodiversity in the Workplace (neurodiversityatwork.com): This website offers a comprehensive range of resources, including articles, case studies, and webinars, specifically tailored to help career coaches navigate the unique challenges and opportunities of supporting neurodiverse individuals in the workplace.
2. The Job Accommodation Network (askjan.org): As a valuable resource for career coaches, this website provides information on workplace accommodations, ADA regulations, and guidance on fostering inclusive environments for neurodiverse individuals. It offers a searchable database of accommodation ideas, case studies, and practical guidance on implementing accommodations in various work settings.
3. Autism Speaks Employment Tool Kit (autismspeaks.org): This toolkit is designed to assist career coaches in supporting individuals on the autism spectrum in their job search and career development. It provides practical advice on topics such as disclosure, interview preparation, and workplace

social skills, along with templates and resources to help individuals with autism succeed in the workplace.

4. Neurodiversity Hub (neurodiversityhub.org): This online platform serves as a hub of information and resources for career coaches working with neurodiverse individuals. It offers articles, research papers, and practical tools to enhance understanding and support the career development of individuals with various neurodivergent conditions.

5. Strengths-based Career Development (strengths-based-careers.com): This website focuses on a strengths-based approach to career coaching for neurodiverse individuals. It provides resources, exercises, and tools that help career coaches identify and leverage the unique strengths and talents of their clients, promoting self-advocacy and empowerment in the career development process.

6. Virtual Job Shadow (virtualjobshadow.com): This online platform offers interactive career exploration tools, including video interviews with professionals in various fields, virtual job tours, and skill-building activities. It is particularly useful for career coaches in helping neurodiverse individuals explore and gain insight into different career paths.

7. Mind Tools (mindtools.com): This website provides a wide range of resources, including articles, quizzes, and tools, to support career coaches in enhancing their coaching skills and helping neurodiverse individuals develop essential employability skills such as time management, communication, and problem-solving.

These websites and tools are invaluable resources for career coaches, educators, human resources professionals, and others involved in supporting the career development of neurodiverse individuals. By utilizing these resources, career coaches can enhance their knowledge, skills, and strategies to empower neurodiverse individuals for career success.

APPENDIX C

Recommended Reading List

As a career coach, educator, human resources professional, or any individual involved in supporting the career development of neurodiverse individuals, it is crucial to stay informed and up-to-date on the latest research, strategies, and insights in the field. This recommended reading list is designed to provide you with a diverse selection of resources primarily focused on career coaching and development for neurodiverse individuals. These books will not only enhance your knowledge but also empower you to effectively embrace the differences and guide your clients towards successful and fulfilling careers.

1. "Neurodiversity in the Workplace: Strength-Based Strategies to Help Employees with Differences Succeed" by Robert D. Austin and Gary P. Pisano

This book explores the concept of neurodiversity and provides practical strategies for creating inclusive work environments. It offers valuable insights into leveraging the strengths of neurodiverse individuals and promoting their success in various career settings.

2. "The Complete Guide to Getting a Job for People with Asperger's Syndrome: Find the Right Career and Get Hired" by Barbara Bissonnette

Specifically tailored for individuals with Asperger's syndrome, this guide offers practical advice on every step of the job-seeking process. From identifying ideal careers to acing interviews and

Printed in Great Britain
by Amazon